GROWING

DOWN

Unlearning *the*

Patterns *of* Adulthood

that Keep Us

from Jesus

Michael Kelley

PUBLISHING GROUP

NASHVILLE, TENNESSEE

Published by B&H Publishing Group
Nashville, Tennessee

Dewey Decimal Classification: 248.84
Subject Heading: ADULTS \ CHRISTIAN LIFE \
SELF-RELIANCE

Cover design and illustration by Wayne Brezinka.

1 2 3 4 5 6 7 • 22 21 20 19 18

For Jana,
Who shows me what it looks like to live in the most
responsibly childlike way. I love you very much.

CONTENTS

CHAPTER 1

Puppy

There is a brown and white puppy with a torn-up right ear that lives in my son's bed. His colors aren't as bright as they used to be; they've faded after a hundred spin cycles in the washing machine, thousands of trips in the car, and nine years of various kinds of stains from various kinds of bodily fluids. It was this same stuffed puppy that my older son, Joshua, clung to during the first few years of his life, when he was being treated for leukemia. It was this same puppy that Joshua then handed down to my daughter, Andi, so she wouldn't be scared to sleep in her big-girl bed. And it's this puppy that was regifted to my youngest son, Christian, to help him say good-bye to his pacifier. That's where the tattered ear comes from—Christian started chewing on the ear at night instead of his pacifier to help him go to sleep.

That puppy's got a lot of baggage on him. Because he does, he's probably more sentimental to my wife and me than to any of our three children at this point. They don't remember all the times Puppy comforted them through pain and heartache and sleeplessness; they don't remember how he was the only thing that would scare the monsters away from under the bed or nurse a sick tummy; they don't remember the heart-exploding sweetness of seeing him passed on from child to child. But we do. And because we do, it's a little sad to know that Puppy's days are numbered in our house.

Our kids are growing up, and as they do, Puppy will eventually go the way of the plastic green army men and dinosaurs. But that's life, right? Like pajamas with characters, Happy Meals, and Disney Junior, Puppy is just another casualty of the reality of the passing years.

Life is about moving from one season to another, and hopefully growing through each one. When you grow, you move past certain things and into other ones. That's true about physical life, but it's also true in a spiritual sense. Both physical life and spiritual life are about growth. In fact, if you're not growing, you're dying.

Born Again

From the moment a baby is conceived, he grows in all different kinds of ways. Within three days of conception, the fertilized egg is dividing rapidly into many cells. Four weeks later, he is already developing a face and neck, as well as a heart, blood vessels, lungs, stomach, and liver. And that baby is just getting started. Once born, a healthy, full-term baby will typically double his birth weight at six months, triple at one year, and almost quadruple before he turns three. Anyone who's ever had that ear-splitting whine wake them up regularly around two or three a.m. knows the baby is hungry because he's growing, and he's growing fast.

It's not that different spiritually.

Problem is, we have been conditioned to think about life in Christ beginning with bowing your head, closing your eyes, and repeating some lines of a prayer led by the preacher at the front of a church or auditorium. I'm not entirely knocking that; we've got to start somewhere. But if that's the only way we think about becoming a Christian, then we are missing the cataclysmic, soul-transforming change that happens inside the heart of that one with his or her head bowed and eyes closed. When Jesus talked about the beginning of that process—when someone moves from darkness to light and death to life—he likened it to being "born again."

Kind of weird, right? Nicodemus thought so, too. He was the scared Pharisee that came to Jesus late one night under the cover of darkness because he was afraid someone would see him talking to this upstart rabbi. He was the one who knocked on the door and whispered in hushed tones, "Rabbi, we know that you are a teacher who has come from God, for no one could perform these signs you do unless God were with him" (John 3:2). When Jesus responded that no one can see the kingdom of God unless he is born again, Nicodemus was a bit confused.

He was a Pharisee after all. He was a child of Israel, a teacher of the law. He thought he knew all about the kingdom of God. He was educated, committed, and respected for his knowledge: "But how can anyone be born when he is old? Can he enter his mother's womb a second time and be born?"

Fair question. A little disgusting, but fair.

Something far less gross, but no less dramatic, would have to happen for life in Christ to begin. Jesus went on to say that entering the kingdom of God is a second birth, one of the Spirit. Just as the wind blows wherever it wills, so does the Spirit, blowing through the dead hearts of mankind and bringing life. With new life comes new . . . everything. A new family. New desires. New loves. New values. Just as a baby in the womb starts growing from the moment of conception,

we, in our new selves in Christ, start the forward progress of growing up in Christ from the moment of our
new birth by the power of the Holy Spirit.

Growing Up

Jesus often used agricultural metaphors in his
teaching. A big reason he did so was simply because
those were the more relatable terms for his audience;
these were people who knew about farming and ranch-
ing. They were people of the land, and that's the language Jesus used to communicate to them. In keeping,
then, with the teaching methodology of Jesus, is the
idea that all living things grow. And as in the case of a
tree, a flower, or an animal, if a person isn't spiritually
growing, they're dying. Take a look at one of the ways
Jesus described life in Christ in John 15:

> "I am the true vine, and my Father is the gar-
> dener. Every branch in me that does not produce
> fruit he removes, and he prunes every branch
> that produces fruit so that it will produce more
> fruit. You are already clean because of the word
> I have spoken to you. Remain in me, and I in
> you. Just as a branch is unable to produce fruit
> by itself unless it remains on the vine, neither
> can you unless you remain in me. I am the vine;
> you are the branches. The one who remains in

me and I in him produces much fruit, because you can do nothing without me." (vv. 1–5)

Jesus, as the vine, is the giver of true life and nourishment. No branch has life on its own; it's only alive to the extent that it is locked in and receiving its life from the vine it's connected to. When that connection is broken, the branch is just a stick, useful for not much else than kindling for a fire. But when the branch remains connected to the vine, the inevitable result is continued and sustained growth that results in fruit. This is far from an isolated text in the New Testament; the Bible shows us over and over that the life of the Christian must be characterized by growth:

- "The righteous thrive like a palm tree and **grow** like a cedar tree in Lebanon" (Ps. 92:12, emphasis added).
- "I planted, Apollos watered, but God gave the **growth**" (1 Cor. 3:6, emphasis added).
- "In him the whole building, being put together, **grows** into a holy temple in the Lord" (Eph. 2:21, emphasis added).
- ". . . until we all reach unity in the faith and in the knowledge of God's Son, **grow**ing into maturity with a stature measured by Christ's fullness" (Eph. 4:13, emphasis added).

- "But speaking the truth in love, let us **grow** in every way into him who is the head—Christ" (Eph. 4:15, emphasis added).
- "And I pray this: that your love will keep on **grow**ing in knowledge and every kind of discernment" (Phil. 1:9, emphasis added).
- ". . . so that you may walk worthy of the Lord, fully pleasing to him: bearing fruit in every good work and **grow**ing in the knowledge of God" (Col. 1:10, emphasis added).
- "Like newborn infants, desire the pure milk of the Word, so that you may **grow** up into your salvation" (1 Pet. 2:2, emphasis added).
- "But **grow** in the grace and knowledge of our Lord and Savior Jesus Christ. To him be the glory both now and to the day of eternity" (2 Pet. 3:18, emphasis added).

In other words, all of us who are in Christ are on the move. We are changing. We are growing. But what is it we are growing into? What does a spiritual adult, in Christ, look like?

Pinocchio and *The Ugly Duckling*

A couple of children's stories might help to explain. Just to refresh your memory, the story of *Pinocchio* begins with a carpenter named Geppetto. Out of his great sadness and loneliness, he constructed a puppet out of wood named Pinocchio (I might have gone to a singles mixer instead). Though it was nice to have the puppet, it just served as a sore reminder of the old man's solitude. So Geppetto wished one night that Pinocchio would not just be a puppet but would come to life, and the Blue Fairy came down and granted his wish. Pinocchio was walking, talking, singing, dancing—the only problem was that he was not a real boy; he was a wooden puppet acting like a real boy. But Pinocchio wanted to be a real boy so badly that he swore he would be the best little boy in the world if the Blue Fairy would turn him from wood to skin. Eventually, Pinocchio gave his own life to save the life of his father, proving that he was worthy to be a real boy, and at last, Pinocchio became what he was always trying to be.

Many of us treat spiritual growth just like that. In our minds, Jesus started something inside of us at that moment we first came into Christ. But in the back of our minds, we are conscious of our own remaining sinfulness and disobedience. It's always there, lurking in the back of our hearts; and over the course of time, we've developed some feelings of guilt, like we should have come much further than we have. We secretly believe that God feels the same way. We know that Jesus made us alive, and like Pinocchio, we can walk, talk, sing, and dance. But we can't fend off our feelings of inadequacy, of despair at our slow progress, of doubt that we'll ever be a "real boy." Our spiritual growth has morphed into a constant compulsion to validate ourselves that inevitably results in bitterness. Like the son who could never throw enough touchdown passes for his all-state quarterback dad, we are the kind of children who are constantly trying to prove ourselves to our heavenly Father.

We are feverishly trying to live up to his standard, and we long for some day out in the future when we'll at long last hear the words, "This is my beloved Son in whom I am well pleased." We are trying, like Pinocchio, to act like what we hope God will make us someday.

That is not the gospel.

That attitude minimizes the work of Jesus on the cross and instead places the burden (and the subsequent glory) on ourselves. We are the wooden puppets bent on achieving rather than the treasured children living gratefully for what we have received.

Our story in the gospel is not like that of Pinocchio; it's more like the story of *The Ugly Duckling*.

You remember that story too, right? Born into a family of ducks, the Ugly Duckling wanted nothing more than to be a regular duck. But no matter how hard he tried, his feathers would not become soft, his quack would not sound right, and his neck would not shrink. He was ridiculed in his duckling-hood because he looked different than the other ducks and was left alone to fend for himself. The real change came one day when the ugly duckling was just about ready to throw in the towel. He gazed morosely into the water and caught a glimpse of his own reflection. His neck wasn't long; it was graceful. His feathers were spread down evenly across his back. He looked almost . . . regal. He realized that he was not a duck, but a swan. Then his actions changed. He flew gracefully. He glided majestically across the water. He was no longer trying to be something else; he had realized who he was all along and then very naturally set on his way to live it out.

Much in the same way, Jesus does not hand us a list of rules and tell us that if we are able to keep them all we will be righteous and therefore suitable for life in the kingdom. Instead, Jesus makes with us a glorious exchange. He takes our sin, and he gives us his own righteousness. And when we choose to accept his offer, the person we once were is uprooted by the Holy Spirit. All our sin is taken away, but we are not left with some gaping hole. Instead, Jesus gives us his righteousness. Suddenly we are not God's enemy; we're his child. We are not criminals, but ambassadors. And he is not our Judge, but our Father. We are changed at the most fundamental of levels, for God made him who had no sin to be sin for us so that we could be the righteousness of God (2 Cor. 5:21). That's at least part of what Paul meant when he said in Romans 8:4 that the righteous requirements of the law have been fully met in us.

Growing in Christ is less about achieving something and more about choosing by faith to live in what Jesus has already achieved on our behalf. In this process, the Holy Spirit leads us to the water over and over again and shows us our new reflection. Then he leans down and whispers, "Remember who you are." As C. S. Lewis put it, "People need to be reminded more than instructed."[1] That's what we are growing up into; we are becoming what we have already become. Growth in Christ is about aligning our thoughts, feelings, and actions to the reality of Christ's finished work in our hearts. But don't let the children's stories fool you. Growing up in Christ is serious business.

Stunted Growth

There is a disease so rare that its mystery extends even into its name. Syndrome X is a condition whereby a child, due to some chromosomal abnormality, simply doesn't grow. They age, in a technical sense, but their mind and body remain the same. Everything except their hair and fingernails exist in a static position of agelessness. And, because there is no growth, there is also a very limited lifespan for those unfortunate enough to suffer from the disease.

Look back at the words of Jesus in John 15. When we remain in him, we grow. And as we grow, we produce fruit. There's really no other option. In fact, Jesus wants in this teaching to make sure we understand that either/or reality: "If anyone does not remain in me, he is thrown aside like a branch and he withers. They gather them, throw them into the fire, and they are burned" (John 15:6).

Grow, or die.

The writer of the book of Hebrews gave us a similar caution. After spending four and a half chapters lifting up the greatness of Jesus, how he is the greater sacrifice and the greater high priest, the writer throws in a rebuke to the audience:

> We have a great deal to say about this, and it's difficult to explain, since you have become too lazy to understand. Although by this time you ought to be teachers, you need someone to teach you the basic principles of God's revelation again. You need milk, not solid food. Now everyone who lives on milk is inexperienced with the message about righteousness, because he is an infant. But solid food is for the mature—for those whose senses have been trained to distinguish between good and evil. Therefore, let us have the elementary teaching about Christ, and go on to maturity, not laying

again a foundation of repentance from dead works, faith in God, teaching about ritual washings, laying on of hands, the resurrection of the dead, and eternal judgment. And we will do this if God permits. (Heb. 5:11–6:3)

I don't know about you, but I feel that warning pretty deeply, especially since the list of things he rattles off in this passage aren't what I would consider to be "beginner" type stuff. But that's part of the problem, isn't it? We have an incredible ability to convince ourselves that we are further along in our spiritual journey than we really are. But these verses from Hebrews shine the mirror of truth on the stunted growth that is epidemic among believers today.

Many in the church seem to be suffering from stunted growth. We are, like those suffering from a spiritual version of Syndrome X, stuck in place on our spiritual journey, not moving forward at all. Our faith is just as it was when we started following Christ. And if these passages are true, we stay in that mode at our peril.

It is as if we are standing in quicksand but don't know it; stuck in one place but content to continue to sink lower and lower until there's nothing left of us at all. But why is that? Why, if the danger is so great and if growth is so natural, do we continue to stay just as we are?

It's not for lack of resources. We are connected as never before. Every book is at our fingertips; churches aren't just on every corner but can be tailor created on a playlist or a virtual community. But despite the abundance of opportunity, there seem to be very few of us actually deepening our walk with Jesus. Richard Foster said it right: "Superficiality is the curse of our age."[2]

Perhaps, despite all our tools, all our metrics, and all our knowledge, there is something we are missing when it comes to spiritual growth. Maybe, in other words, growing up in Christ doesn't look exactly like we think it does. This is where a great irony comes into play. In order to grow up in Christ, we must actually choose to grow down.

Children of the Kingdom

Picture the scene with me. It's another busy day in the life of Jesus. His reputation has spread; he scarcely has a moment to himself anymore. Everywhere he and his disciples turn, there are people. Sick people. Needy people. Accusing people. Skeptical people. And, on this particular day, there are also a bunch of kids.

It seemed parents in the crowd had started pushing and shoving their way forward with their kiddos in tow. They were coming because it was customary in those days for a great teacher of the law to lay his hands on children and pray for them in order to bless them. That's just what these parents were doing. They, like Nicodemus, didn't quite know what to make of Jesus, but they had seen and heard enough to know they wanted to get their rug rats some of that blessing he might be handing out.

Jesus' disciples didn't want any part of it. In fact, the disciples "rebuked" these tiger parents and their disruptive kiddos (Matt. 19:13). That's a strong word—rightly so. There was nothing polite about what the disciples did; it's not as if they pulled Mom and Dad aside and quietly whispered, "Jesus is actually teaching right now, but we're going to have a meet-and-greet later and you are more than welcome to come then." This word is so strong, in fact, that in another form it can be translated, "punished."

I can relate, I suppose. I remember a couple of years ago when Jana and I took our three children (then nine, six, and four years old) to the most magical place on Earth. I remember going through the turnstile and being greeted by plants resembling cartoon dogs and ducks and the familiar refrain of "It's a Small World." We stood for a moment, looking at the gates of the Magic Kingdom at Disney World, and then the terrible reality hit me: *We're here too early.*

That wasn't the plan. I had clocked it out. My goal was to arrive anywhere from two to seven minutes early because I knew arriving any earlier would result in anarchy. And yet there we stood, forty-two minutes prior to gate opening.

That's forty-two minutes in the unshaded heat. Forty-two minutes with three kids and two iPhones. Forty-two minutes of nowhere to sit except the Floridian concrete. Forty-two minutes of looking at the promise of fun and adventure and not being able to go in. And after about seventeen seconds, the kids let us know:

"When is it going to open?" *Forty-two minutes.*

"Why can't we go in?" *It's not open yet.*

"How come those people are going in?" *Because they are staying at a hotel on site.*

"Our hotel stinks! I want to stay at that hotel!" *Get a job.*

In that moment, I could have done with an entourage of my own disciples bent on protecting me from the kids. That's what the disciples did—they formed a verbal and punitive wall around Jesus, and ironically, they did it to *protect* him.

Jesus is too busy for that kid. He's too important to spend time like this. He shouldn't have to deal with these trivialities. If you only knew him like we do, you wouldn't be so quick to bring your snotty brats this close.

Funny how we do that sometimes, isn't it? Try and protect Jesus? We do it in the marketplace and in debates; we do it in the culture and with the skeptic. We are like Peter, drawing our sword and waving it at any old ear that needs to be cut off, like the Son of God isn't capable of protecting himself.

Jesus, in response to the protection of the disciples, is even more incensed than they were at this intrusion: "When Jesus saw it, he was indignant and said to them, 'Let the little children come to me'" (Mark 10:14).

Now, Jesus got frustrated with his disciples a lot. He was disappointed in their level of understanding several times. But this is the only time in the Bible where he is "indignant" with them. Evidently, there was something about this whole scene, chaotic as it undoubtedly was, that made the Son of God really, really angry.

There are a lot of conclusions we can draw about that. We can know, for example, that there is a special place in the heart of Jesus for children. We can also know that Jesus loved the parents, and he knew that denying the children meant casting away Mom and Dad. And we can know that Jesus was angry because no one—not even the smallest baby—is outside of his providential care.

But we can also see from here that Jesus was angry because the disciples had missed something crucial about the nature of the kingdom of God and what it means to receive it: "Don't stop them, because the kingdom of God belongs to such as these. Truly I tell you, whoever does not receive the kingdom of God like a little child will never enter it" (Mark 10:14–15).

It seems that for all the growing in knowledge, understanding, and proximity to Jesus the disciples had done, they really hadn't moved much past square one. In fact, these children were closer to understanding what it means to come to Jesus and embrace his kingdom than the disciples were. The same thing is true for us.

Childish and Childlike Faith

If we want to grow up in Jesus, then it seems we must grow down and become more like children. But that presents a problem, doesn't it? What I mean is, it seems that the Bible combines faith and children in both a positive and a negative way. In the passage above, it's clearly positive. Jesus says that the kingdom of heaven is made up of people like the children. And yet Paul seemed to argue just the opposite: "When I was a child, I spoke like a child, I thought like a child, I reasoned like a child. When I became a man, I put aside childish things" (1 Cor. 13:11). It seems like the Bible is speaking out of both sides of its mouth, or at least that Jesus and Paul disagree. Jesus was teaching that entering the kingdom of heaven is about having faith like a child;

Paul seems to say that growing in Christ is about putting away childish ways.

Let's frame it another way—maybe there is a difference between "childlike" faith and "childish" faith. That is to say, a childish faith is a mark of immaturity as a Christ-follower. But childlike faith is a mark of depth. In fact, you could perhaps say that the disciples were marked by childish faith, and what they needed was to become more like the very ones they were so eager to turn away.

If that's true, it begs the question of what it means to come to God over and over again as a child might. But to get to the end of that trail, where we really know what it means to grow up in Christ by growing down, let's see if we can find out what it is about being an adult in the eyes of the world that might keep us from truly embracing and experiencing the fullness of who Jesus is and what it's like to live in his kingdom.

CHAPTER 2

UNLEARNING ADULTHOOD

The Grown-up Life

What does it mean to be an adult? It depends on who you ask. Our kids, for instance, for some time, have believed that life in the Kelley home shuts down around eight p.m. This isn't far from the truth; I don't like to stay up much past the average seven-year-old. That being said, my wife and I actually have real conversations and a generally pretty good time after the kids are in bed.

Recently, though, they've started to peek behind the curtain of bedtime, driven by the curiosity of just what happens when the prayers are said, the last drink is had, and the kisses are generously distributed.

Our home, which was built in the late 1950s, is creaky. If you're upstairs and you are interested in a clandestine trip out of your bed, you're pretty much out of luck. The old people on the lower level are going to hear you coming. So we know by the sound of short-strided footsteps that there is a little person coming to the top of the stairs trying to get a peek at what Mom and Dad are doing down there, away from them, all by themselves. Usually it's not too exciting. Maybe a movie. Probably a snack and a soda. Because, you know, that's what adults do.

If you asked my kids, then, what it means to be an adult, they would tell you plainly: "It means you get to stay up late and eat popcorn and drink soda." Fair enough, young ones. But if you asked another set of kids from another family in another place the same question, you'd likely get a very different answer.

If, for example, you asked a child from the Okiek tribe in Kenya what it means to be an adult, they would describe a ritualistic rite of passage. In that culture, the young boys and girls are secluded from the adults for several months. During that time, they paint themselves white using clay in order to take on the appearance of a wild creature. Then, each night, they are stalked by a "mythical creature" they only recognize because of its distinct roar. They become adults when the elders of the tribe show them the instrument they were using to produce the roar, so they in turn can create the sound for themselves.

If you asked any number of aboriginal tribes in Australia what it means to be an adult, they might describe the walkabout. That's when young men are sent into the wilderness for up to six months to see if they are truly ready to become men. Their goal? Survival. Completely isolated and unassisted. When—and if—they come back, they are considered the men of the tribe.

Then there is the Sateré-Mawé tribe in the Brazilian Amazon, who participate in their own coming-of-age ritual when they turn thirteen. In this "Bullet and Ant" initiation, the young people search the jungle for bullet ants. The ants are then sedated by putting them into an herbal solution before they are woven into gloves with the stingers pointed inward. When the ants wake up, they are understandably upset, and that's when the initiation begins. Each boy is required to wear the gloves for ten minutes to show their readiness for manhood. What's more, they have to put the gloves back on as many as twenty times over several months to show they are truly grown up.

I guess a soda and a snack really is something to look forward to.

The question of what and when defines adulthood has been interpreted in different ways at different times by different people. In recent years in the United States, we've seen the age of adulthood steadily pushed back due to any number of reasons—many of them economical. The biggest reason for this delay, according to the Pew Research Center, is the inability to find a job. A study conducted in August of 2010 showed evidence that each of the five milestones of adulthood—completing school, leaving home, becoming financially independent, marrying, and having a child—have been pushed later and later. [3]

This makes defining adulthood really tough. It's a moving target, determined on a generational basis and informed by everything from cultural expectations to the economic outlook. Rather than looking to a specific age, then, we should ask whether there is a primary trait that characterizes the shift from child to adult. Is there something common, regardless of generation and culture, that, when a person is "like this," he or she is no longer a child?

I think there is. And I think that "something" is self-sufficiency. It's the ability to make their own decisions, earn their own money, and exist apart from the help of others. Graduation into adulthood is moving into independence so you can responsibly decide what time you go to bed and how many bowls of popcorn you want to eat.

Now I know my kids think it's glamorous, but it's not all soda and later bedtimes. I remember the sheer panic I felt when, at twenty, I got married and suddenly realized that I had no idea how to pay an electric bill or whether I needed life insurance. (For the record, I have since learned the answer to both of those questions. Mostly.)

This transition is a good thing. We need to grow up, today more than ever. Big boys need to start understanding what it means to be men. They need to love and treasure responsibility and commitment and embrace their role in the church and society at large. Little girls need to understand what it means to be strong women who are willing to follow as well as lead and display their strength and fortitude of character in both instances. We need, as a culture, to grow up.

Mostly.

Let's take it back to that base definition of growing up. If growing up is mainly about self-sufficiency and self-reliance, then we have a very serious problem, because the gospel runs diametrically opposed to both of those things. The gospel is, first and foremost, about acknowledging that you can't take care of yourself. That you are, in fact, absolutely powerless to do anything to change your sinful condition, and you are therefore in great need. You are helpless . . . like a child.

The Swiss theologian Emil Brunner once said, "All other religions spare us the ultimate humiliation of being stripped naked and being declared bankrupt before God."[4] That's pretty strong language.

And yet it points to the humiliating nature of Christianity. None of the other world religions treat humanity with such pessimism. In all other schools of thought, we have something to bring to the table. We can strive toward God and meet him and, in a sense, be congratulated when we do.

Not Christianity.

In Christianity, we bring nothing to the table. In fact, the only thing we bring to the equation of salvation is the sin we need to be rescued from. Perhaps that's why, if we look back into history, Christianity has been called the religion of women and slaves. In cultures of the past, neither of those two groups had many rights, so it wasn't a far stretch for them to admit their abject need of God's complete and total intervention on their behalf. This is one of the reasons why Jesus said it was difficult for the rich to come into the kingdom—because with the wealth of possessions comes the difficulty of owning our poverty of soul. There is the ever-increasing tendency to rely on our stuff for our security instead of throwing ourselves empty-handed at the foot of the cross. This willing humiliation is a prerequisite in coming to Jesus, for all are welcome at the foot of the cross except those who don't really think they need to be there.

Christianity cuts the knees before it lifts the soul.

See the problem? The universal characteristic of adulthood—self-sufficiency—is the same characteristic that keeps us from Jesus. And that's just the beginning of the problem. As we grow, we develop all manners of thinking and behavior that might make us very good citizens of our culture, but very poor children of the kingdom of God.

Accumulation

Let me take you back to the story of Jesus and the children. It's one of the rare stories that appears not once, not twice, but three times in three Gospels. If you look back at all three accounts in Matthew, Mark, and Luke, you'll find that each writer records Jesus' encouragement to actually become like the children he so freely welcomed. Then each account is followed in the exact same way—with the story of the rich, young ruler:

> As he was setting out on a journey, a man ran up, knelt down before [Jesus], and asked him, "Good teacher, what must I do to inherit eternal life?"

"Why do you call me good?" Jesus asked him. "No one is good but God alone. You know the commandments: Do not murder; do not commit adultery; do not steal; do not bear false witness; do not defraud; honor your father and mother."

He said to him, "Teacher, I have kept all these from my youth."

Looking at him, Jesus loved him and said to him, "You lack one thing: Go, sell all you have and give to the poor, and you will have treasure in heaven. Then come, follow me." But he was dismayed by this demand, and he went away grieving, because he had many possessions. (Mark 10:17–22)

Now there's a guy who had it all. Wealth, prestige, and power—a respectable member of the community. Not only that, but apparently he had the moral fortitude to go along with it. And yet, after coming to Jesus, he went away sad. Much sadder, I dare say, than those kiddos who scampered up to the Son of God a few verses earlier.

Why is that? It's because Jesus told him that if he wanted to come into the kingdom, he had to sell everything he had. To become poor. And that made him sad, because he had a lot of stuff.

That's the way adulthood works. As we age, we accumulate. We accumulate material possessions, sure, but along with those material possessions we accumulate other things. Other attitudes. Other experiences. Other wounds. Growing up is about accumulation.

Think of it like a set of luggage. When you're young, you've got very little in your suitcase. Your only experience with the world is with your parents, who for the most part, kept you a bit sheltered from things that would harm you. As far as you knew, the milk would never run out, the people would never be mean and cruel, and the worst thing that would ever happen to you could be fixed with a brightly colored Band-Aid to the knee. But then, and for some more quickly than others, you start accumulating experiences that teach you otherwise.

There's the first time your parent loses his or her patience with you and the harsh word comes. That gets stored in your little suitcase, always with you to remember.

Or maybe someone close to you, either by their words or actions, teaches you that relationships don't last forever. They leave, and you start wondering for the first time whether or not you are actually worth staying for. That fills up the suitcase pretty nicely, and you find you actually have to get another one.

Then comes the moment when you realize you're not as beautiful or talented as you once thought, and that moment comes not through kindness but through cruelty. Stock that one away in the suitcase for later, too.

Pretty soon your one suitcase has turned into a matched set and you are lugging all your disappointments, heartaches, and notions about the world and the God who supposedly reigns over it, and the baggage is pretty heavy. Much heavier than when you started.

The really interesting part, though, is that you have a love/hate relationship with this luggage. You hate it because it's so cumbersome to drag around all the time. It weighs on your mind and soul day after day. It encumbers your soul, colors your relationships, and distorts your outlook for tomorrow. But you love it, too, because you have had it so long you don't even know who you are without it. It's what makes you distinct. It's what makes you "special." This luggage is a part of your core identity.

Then, into this bunker of accumulation, Jesus drops the grenade of voluntary loss. This is exactly what he did to the rich, young ruler, who had his own set of accumulated suitcases. "Come to me," he says. "But don't come with your hands full. Put down the luggage."

That's when your heart starts beating a little faster, just as the rich, young ruler's did. Sell it all? Get rid of it? Declutter and unencumber yourself? Part of that choice feels so simple and appealing—just drop the luggage and come to Jesus. But the actual dropping is hard. Your back has grown strong. It feels weird not to have all these bags hanging off of you. It feels open, exposed, naked—and you begin to waver because some part of you genuinely feels that you not only want all that baggage; you actually need it.

But this voluntary loss is the pathway to great gain; the unencumbering of our souls frees us to be filled up by Jesus. Intimacy with Jesus means willingly letting go of that which we have filled our lives with along the way. Jesus, for the sake of the relationship with us that he desires so much, is calling us to declutter ourselves from things like complexity and self-reliance. He's calling us to sell off our privacy and our anxiety. He wants to free us from education and apathy, from self-consciousness and busyness. All these characteristics are filling the bags draped around our shoulders, and their weight makes us turn away again and again from what Jesus is offering.

Unlearning Adulthood

Let's play out the story of the rich, young ruler a little more. To our knowledge, the story ends with the man going away sad. He walked despondently back to his big house and sat in the middle of his big things. He was surrounded by all the carefully curated comforts that once made him feel so safe, secure, and stable, but had, over the course of time, lost their luster in the face of what he was lacking.

But what if the story didn't end there? What if he changed his mind? What if, later that evening, after this encounter with Jesus, the very things he once treasured started to rise like bile in his spirit? Maybe they did, and maybe he decided right then and there to do exactly what Jesus told him. So he began the task that took him all night long, going through his house and tagging and marking for sale everything he found there. Then early the next morning he held the yard sale of all yard sales. He put everything he owned in front of his house and hailed the entire community with calls of "Everything must go! Rock-bottom prices!" And one by one, people curiously wandered up, shocked to see that they could have these luxuries at little to no cost. And with every sale, the young man's countenance brightened. The piles got lower. The stuff got thinner. Until after a solid morning of peddling his treasures, he had only one set of meager clothes and a pile of cash that he promptly walked around giving away. And now, unencumbered by the weight of his baggage, he ran again, but faster this time, because he had to catch up to Jesus.

Can you imagine that next meeting? It would have been much different than the day before. I suspect there would have been a lightness to it; a winsomeness that was absent from the desperation the young man carried with him previously. For now, the young man was ready to start following Jesus, but it would have been just the start.

Even though the man, in this imaginative scenario, did sell everything he owned and did start following Jesus, he was only at the beginning of his journey. What would come after was the same thing that still comes to all of us who follow Jesus: unlearning.

This man, like all of us, would have grown up in a system of thinking that needed to be engaged, confronted, and then reshaped. We have been educated in self-actualization, materialism, anxiety, and accumulation, and we have to unlearn these things to truly experience the kingdom of God. This unlearning is an intentional effort on our part to recognize that the things that make us mature in the eyes of the world actually hold us back from maturity in the eyes of God. Fortunately for us, though, Jesus is really good at helping people unlearn things.

Think back to Jesus' most famous sermon, the Sermon on the Mount. The people would have been jammed together, either sitting on the ground or maybe even standing, for it was customary in those days for the teacher to sit and the audience to stand. Probably not a whole lot of shade from the hot sun, either. What might have made it even more uncomfortable were the people in attendance.

If we look back a couple of chapters in the Bible to Matthew 4, we get a good picture of the rabble that was following Jesus:

> Then the news about him spread throughout Syria. So they brought to him all those who were afflicted, those suffering from various diseases and intense pains, the demon-possessed, the epileptics, and the paralytics. And he healed them. Large crowds followed him from Galilee, the Decapolis, Jerusalem, Judea, and beyond the Jordan. (Matt. 4:24–25)

Jesus, even this early in his ministry, was developing quite a following. And a reputation. People were coming out of the woodwork, in large part because this man was healing the sick and associating with people no one else would. He spoke with authority and loved generously. What do we think, then, that the crowds looked like as they sat on the hill that day? Suits and ties? Sundresses?

There was no polite listening here. No nicely dressed parishioners with Moleskine notebooks and coffee cups in hand. Imagine men and women, shunned by society because of their physical ailments. Their sin. Their injuries. Their reputations. Illnesses of all kinds.

Imagine the words of Jesus being interrupted by an epileptic seizure, or the shrieks of the demon-possessed. While you're at it, consider the smell. Rotting flesh. Clothes dug out of garbage heaps. The scent, almost palpable, of people who have been discarded as unimportant, unnecessary, and unclean by society.

But Jesus looks at the crowd and smiles, for these are the people, so neglected and unloved, who are also so ready to hear the good news. So he begins to teach them, never once holding his nose.

Jesus taught them about the nature of the kingdom of God, how in this kingdom, everything is flipped on its head. Up is down. Left is right. Poor is rich. Hungry is full. Persecuted is blessed. He taught about how these people are salt and light to the rest of the world when they believe in him. He taught them that their skin conditions and palsies and injuries and poverty were not the measure of their righteousness or purity.

He was helping them unlearn—reeducating them according to the values, priorities, and patterns of thinking of his kingdom. And he didn't stop there.

How many times in his ministry did Jesus set his hearers up for this very dynamic of unlearning with the simple phrase, "You have heard it said . . . but I say to you . . ."

Jesus is inviting us, once again, to come face-to-face with what we have heard, and then find that what he says is the exact opposite. Because he has invited us, I want to invite you, too, to come to the Master of Reeducation and humbly ask him to help us, through the course of these pages, to grow down in all the important ways so that we might grow up in him. What might happen if we unlearned these patterns of behavior and instead replaced them with those attributes that once upon a time came so naturally to us, before the world had its way in our lives? What if we moved from self-reliance to dependence? From complexity to simplicity? From privacy to authenticity? From anxiety to trust? From education to wonder? From apathy to passion? From busyness to rest?

We would, spiritually speaking, be a lot less like adults who have life completely figured out, and more like children who are grateful to be with Jesus. And then we would find Jesus not saying, "Go, sell everything you have," but instead, "Let them come to Me."

CHAPTER 3

The Perils of Bathtime

Thanks, Facebook and Instagram. Though you have a lot of great perks, I especially appreciate the moments that remind me of my failings as a parent. I take a look at you and realize that my kids must be the only ones who misbehave, throw tantrums, and are excessively needy.

Take bathtime, for example. If social media is to be believed, it's all water fights and cutely placed bubble beards. Not at the Kelley house. It's a battle for parental sanity because we live in a house that's not friendly to kid-directed bathing.

Our home has a lot of the original fixtures. It hasn't yet been updated in the kids' bathroom with the easy-on, easy-off, hot-is-red, and blue-is-cold kind of faucet. Instead, there are two knobs that have to be turned at precisely the right moment and positioned at precisely the right trajectory to harmonize the perfect amount of hot and cold water coming out of the faucet. If you're too aggressive, you've either got a child screaming like they've just been laid bare backed on the July sidewalk or howling like they're ice fishing in Minnesota. My life at bathtime is the constant back and forth between bathroom and living room, slightly turning the hot and cold knobs first this way, then that way, until gradually the hot water is all gone along with the remnants of my patience.

But there's hope. Gloriously, our kids have now mostly aged into the realm of self-directed showers, and the dawn comes with the morning.

That's part of what growing up is, isn't it? It's learning to do things for yourself. You gradually learn how to cook food, make your bed, and do your own laundry (though for some of us, it comes later than others, and it's still a work in progress). Independence is a good thing; it's a necessary thing. As we parent our children, we move toward the end of releasing them into the world, and one of the litmus tests of whether we've done our job or not is just how well they can function out there in that big, wide world on their own.

But self-reliance is a slippery slope. While self-reliance is good and right for the way we function in the world, it is a very poor characteristic for the child of God. In fact, self-reliance actually runs contrary to the gospel.

The Slippery Slope of Self-Reliance

The core of the gospel is hinged on an understanding of our complete and utter powerlessness. While the message of every other spiritual system is essentially "you can," the beginning of understanding Christianity is wholeheartedly embracing the crushing reality that "you can't." The reason you can't is not because you're not smart enough, wise enough, or strong enough. Your inability (along with every other human in history) is a function of the state of your being. Like so many other facets of our relationship with God, though, we tend to pay lip service to this truth, even while our lives and attitudes show our insufficient grasp of it.

I remember, for example, a preacher from my childhood who wove an illustration with vivid imagery that caused many to walk to the front of the auditorium. The word picture went like this:

Imagine yourself stranded at sea. There is no boat in sight, no piece of driftwood to hold you up. Just you and the water. Sure, you've had some swim lessons, but you're no fool—you know that in this vast ocean there is only so long you can tread water. The minutes start to tick by, one by one, and with each second you know that your strength is a little bit less than it was before. Then you notice that your kicking legs are starting to feel heavy. You tilt your head back as you realize that you're starting to sink deeper. Now your ears are almost fully submerged. You know the end is close, and then suddenly you take on that first bit of water. You cough it up and your heart begins to race. You come to the sudden realization that there is no hope for you. Your head dips again and you prepare yourself to swallow, when suddenly, out of nowhere, you see the rope being thrown your way. With your last ounce of strength, you grab it, and you are pulled to safety.

That is what it means to be saved. Jesus, when you couldn't save yourself, tosses you a line at the cross. Just reach up and grab it, and he will pull you to safety.

I get it. This particular preacher inspired a sense of danger and urgency in the hearts and minds of his hearers, and God was faithful to use what he said to awaken the need for Jesus in many hearts. There's really only one problem with the illustration: We get way too much credit.

In contrast, this is how the Bible describes all of humanity:

> And you were dead in your trespasses and sins in which you previously lived according to the ways of this world, according to the ruler of the power of the air, the spirit now working in the disobedient. We too all previously lived among them in our fleshly desires, carrying out the inclinations of our flesh and thoughts, and we were by nature children under wrath as the others were also. (Eph. 2:1–3)

You've got to hand it to Paul the apostle—he doesn't pull any punches. There's not a silver lining in that cloud. Notice the specific word the Bible used to describe the human condition: dead. If that word doesn't speak to the severity and desperation of our situation, then surely nothing does. In fact, this word moves our situation well past desperate and into the territory of hopeless.

Nobody goes to a funeral and stands around chit-chatting only to point up to the front of the church and ask his friends, "I wonder what Frank is going to do this weekend?" That's because Frank is dead. And when you're dead, you're dead. Game over. In fact, "deadness" is a condition that renders someone incapable of changing anything about their situation. The only change comes when and if an outside force acts upon them to move them into a different state than they currently are.

This isn't a picture of someone drowning, taking on water. Instead, the picture here is of a corpse, dead and bloated, floating face down in the sea. No strength. No power. No hope.

That's the beginning of understanding the gospel. Without that beginning, a person might be able to have a positive attitude, look on the bright side, and say some encouraging things to others—but they'll never be right with God. They'll never be truly alive.

Enter Jesus. Ephesians 2 continues with two of the most amazing words in all of Scripture: "But God . . ." We were dead, but God . . . We had no hope, but God . . . We could not rescue ourselves, but God . . .

The gospel doesn't claim to help the weak; it claims to make the dead live again. It is only when we begin to see the true nature of the utter despair of humanity that we begin to see Jesus not as the key to a better life, not as a sage only teaching about love, and not as a miracle worker only concerned with the alleviation of human suffering, but as the true Savior.

Jesus is our Rescuer. And, according to the Bible, he rescues from sin and death. In the ultimate "But God" moment, Jesus jumps into the sea of sin and death and hauls our lifeless bodies to the shore. Then, he leans low, and breathes new life into us. What was dead lives. Glory to God, and glory to God alone.

All throughout Scripture, the helplessness of humanity is highlighted to cast the spotlight on the greatness of God. No matter how noble, how courageous, how strong, or how faithful an individual might be, the Bible makes a point to show us that alongside any of those positive character traits exists the helpless, frail, frightened individual that, no matter how much they grow, still stands in need.

David was a man after God's own heart, a great songwriter, and the greatest king over Israel. He was a faithful friend, a tremendous leader, and not bad with a slingshot. He was also a bad father, an adulterer, and a murderer.

Scripture calls Moses the humblest man who ever lived. He talked with God face-to-face as a man talks to a man, and he stood in front of the most powerful man on the planet and boldly proclaimed the word of the Lord. He also killed a man and was prevented from entering the Promised Land due to his brashness and lack of faith.

Abraham was the father of God's chosen people, and even when the New Testament was written he was held up as a model of faith. He did not withhold his only son from the Lord. But he also believed in God so little that he passed his wife off as his sister for fear of being killed by the Egyptians.

The list goes on. Peter denied Christ. Samson had a head too big to fit in a building. Gideon was a coward. We can only conclude that the Bible is very concerned that as we look upon the greatness of its characters, we also see their failures. In light of that, there really are no heroes in the Bible, save one: God, and God incarnate Jesus Christ. Humans aren't the saviors; they're the ones that need saving.

It is by grace alone, through faith alone, that we become right with God and walk intimately with him. Prerequisite to receiving grace is seeing your need. A child doesn't have that issue. A child knows without knowing he or she is helpless. And while bathtime might be a frustrating endeavor from the perspective of a parent, it's also a reminder that this little person is in need, is not self-reliant, and is dependent on someone stronger than she is. Given those things, are you starting to see how growing into a self-reliant adult might unintentionally fracture a relationship that is built on your need and God's provision? Let me, then, describe two manifestations of our self-reliance: our quest for security and our loss of helplessness.

The Quest for Security

I want my children to feel safe. We've tried to make our home a place where our kids know they can always come—a place where they will be taken care of. That's part, I believe, of what God has entrusted me to do as their father. I am to mirror his greater provision and security for them so that when they hear him say, "I will take care of you," they will have a starting point for beginning that understanding. By God's grace, I pray that they might think of God and his care like this: "It's like Daddy, but better."

God loves me like Daddy does . . . only better.

God provides for me like Daddy does . . . only better.

God disciplines me like Daddy does . . . only better.

God takes care of me like Daddy does . . . only better.

If only it worked exactly like that. At some point in all our lives, we make the shift from assuming security to seeking security. For some, that shift happens into adolescence, but for others, it happens much, much earlier. Maybe you, from a very early age, know what it's like to carry the burden of your own security. Maybe your father or mother long ago, either by their physical or emotional absence, left that burden on your shoulders. You were the one who didn't have the luxury of concerning yourself with whether you would get picked first or last in kickball; you were too busy worrying about whether or not you would be safe at night when the door closed or whether there would be anyone there when you woke up in the morning.

Regardless of when that transition happens, all of us make it, and when we do, we spend a great amount of time and resources as adults trying to make ourselves feel secure. We buy insurance policies, invest in 401Ks, cultivate emergency funds, avoid the wrong kind of fats (whichever those are this week), and put on our seat belts, all to try and regain the simple security that we once had when we didn't even think twice about whether or not there would be dinner on the table at night.

Notice, though, I said we *try* to make ourselves feel secure, because security is really only an illusion. The stock market will crash. The car wreck will happen. The diagnosis will come. The relationship will end. And when those things happen, all of our carefully constructed straw houses of security will be blown down with the winds of circumstance. The best we can hope for is that our personal illusion holds up as long as possible under the weight of the world.

That quest for security is the manifestation of our self-reliance regardless of our spiritual beliefs. We all need it, and we all do it. And security for adults becomes the elephant in the room—the thing that we're constantly seeking and yet all of us know is tee-tering on the edge of nonexistence at any moment.

But there is another manifestation of our drift towards self-reliance that is particular to Christians. It's the slow but steady pull we feel away from that initial truth of the gospel that emphasizes our powerlessness. We move from being cognizant of our great need and toward a form of religion whereby we consider our-selves saved by grace, and yet we trust in our own works to keep us in God's good graces moving forward. This "Christian legalism" is sanitized self-reliance. It's the story of the Galatian church.

The Loss of Helplessness

Paul started the churches in Galatia on some very simple principles, but they all boiled down to this: A relationship with God is built on faith in Jesus Christ and his finished work at the cross. No more, no less. And the people embraced that message. They built their lives around it. They turned to this system of religious thought and began to do their business, raise their families, and turn their thinking toward Jesus as the center of the universe. But then, as he was apt to do as a church-planter, Paul left.

One day, some new characters came walking into the towns and cities of Galatia. These people looked a lot like Paul, they talked about many of the same things that Paul did, and they even seemed to be as educated as Paul. They, like Paul, said they had a message for the people about God and Jesus. But theirs was a little different in some subtle but important ways.

The message of these new teachers was that while faith in Jesus was a good thing, to be truly right with God, they had to combine that faith with certain actions. They claimed that anyone who wanted to be in right relationship with God must practice certain religious holidays, abstain from certain foods, and most importantly, undergo circumcision.

Keep in mind that the Galatians weren't converted Jews; they were Gentiles. Circumcision was a Jewish rite and always had been. It was a mark in Israel of those belonging to their community. History calls these teachers in the Galatian region Judaizers, because their message was that the pathway to God was not just through Christ; it was to actually become Jewish, then believe in Christ, and then be right with God.

The end result was that a portion—maybe even the majority—of the Galatians believed their message and began following this new teaching. Eventually the apostle got word of what was happening there, and he wrote a letter that we have in our Bibles as the book of Galatians. Paul dealt with the issue in a decisive fashion.

Paul began his letter not with a flowery prayer, as he often did in his correspondence, but instead with these words: "I am amazed that you are so quickly turning away from him who called you by the grace of Christ and are turning to a different gospel" (Gal. 1:6). Amazed. Shocked. Bumfuzzled. Flummoxed. Flabbergasted. And that's just the beginning.

In that letter, we find Paul using some of the harshest language we find anywhere in the Bible. Throughout the six chapters, he called them stupid and foolish; he claimed they hated freedom and loved the law; he even said that he hoped that any false teachers would simply go to hell. It is a scathing rebuke, one that might cause us, at least in the back of our minds to wonder, *Aren't you overreacting a little? I mean, it's not like they're denying that Jesus existed. It's certainly not that they're adopting a different kind of God. It's just a bodily operation, for goodness' sake. Is it really that big of a deal?* And the answer to that question is a resounding yes. It is that big of a deal. That's because the loss of our own sense of helplessness is the abandonment of the gospel.

It IS That Big of a Deal

These false teachers were putting the souls of the Galatians at risk when they convinced the Galatians that they weren't as helpless as they thought.

Paul was shocked that they were "deserting" the gospel. The phrase there literally means a transfer of allegiance. In other literature, it was used of army deserters—of traitors. Those who change their loyalty. Paul didn't say they were altering or amending; he said they were changing from one side to another. Instead of trusting in Christ alone for their salvation, they were transferring their trust from Christ to themselves. It was no longer that "Jesus has saved me"; it was instead a team effort. So when we, like the Galatians, start to believe that we are not truly helpless, we are actually becoming traitors to the gospel. That leads to the second great thing at risk here: the glory of the Son of God.

Can you imagine looking to the cross of Jesus Christ, the perfect Son of God slain for sinful humanity, and saying, "That's almost enough"? Saying, "It's a pretty good job, but not quite there"? And can you further imagine the audacity to say that we, by some bodily operation, somehow complete the goodness of that sacrifice? And yet this is precisely what the Galatians did, and precisely what we also drift toward.

As we get older, we become more independent and self-reliant. When we apply that same tendency to the gospel, we drift slowly with our age out of the beauty of helplessness and into the illusion of self-care until we wake up one day convinced that we are just fine on our own.

As Christians, we will always fight against the temptation to make ourselves feel better about ourselves. It's the temptation to insulate ourselves against our true need manifested in the form of self-justification. In this battle, we must take an active stance not to grow up in our ability to fend for ourselves, but to instead return to that level ground at the foot of the cross. We don't have to drift toward self-reliance; we can instead choose to grow down, day after day, into the childlike dependence on a Father who alone justifies us. But how do we take this active stance? How do we grow down in our self-reliance and grow up in our dependence on God? It's simpler than you think.

Our Daily Bread

We can start with prayer.

Prayer is about communion with God. Though we might tend to treat it more like a magic lamp, prayer is a gift whereby we can actually communicate with God in an intimate way. When Jesus' disciples came to him and asked him about prayer, he laid out a pattern that was nothing short of revolutionary. Whereas these men had been reared in a system emphasizing the esteem and reverence rightly paid to God, Jesus helped them see that there was a way they could hold that same God in an even higher esteem, not through separation, but through intimacy. He did this through the use of a single word: Father.

This Father who is in heaven still has a name that should be hallowed. But in that respect for his name to be made great, we find not fear, but love. And Jesus wasn't done yet. Read down a few verses, to the first time in that model prayer that Jesus told his followers to pray something for themselves, and you find this:

"Give us each day our daily bread . . ."

There are two aspects to that single request that jump out to me. First of all, there is a sense of helplessness built into it. Bread is not extravagant; it was the staple of life in the first century. And yet in this prayer, the one praying is acknowledging that even this, the most basic of all things, is still a gift that comes from the hand of God. What's more, we are to pray this *daily*. Not our weekly bread; not our monthly bread; but our daily bread. What we find in this is a pattern of disciplined self-reminding that helps us remember our own helplessness. The simple act of asking, again and again, serves to remind us that we are people not of sufficiency but of great need. That's one of the most basic ways we can grow in our dependence on God— through daily asking him for our daily bread, whatever that daily bread happens to be for that particular day.

The great news of this prayer, and for the Christian who lives in the awareness of his need, is that we are to ask like children confident of the love of our Father. We ask knowing that he has an inexhaustible supply of bread for his children, and he is not stingy in passing it out on a daily basis. That's the truly glorious news of our helplessness.

If we aren't convinced of the goodness of God, our helplessness is cause for great alarm. But if, on the other hand, we could be absolutely sure that God is not only powerful but also loving, then helplessness is exactly where we want to be. That's because when we are in need, we get the provision, and God gets the glory as the provider.

But how can we know that God will not hang us out to dry? How can we know he will not be like an earthly father who might indeed give us a snake when we ask for a fish? How can we get past our self-reliance and move joyfully into disciplined dependence like the dearly loved children of a parent with limitless resources?

It is by looking to the cross, where God proved his love for us. When we come there—that level ground of the cross, where we see that no one has a leg up—and acknowledge our desperate need, we over and over again feel the freedom of the words of Jesus Christ. They are the words that contradict the Judaizers' message in Galatians. They are the words that trump our need for self-justification. They are the words that remind us that it's actually the best news in the world that we are helpless. They are the words that direct all the misplaced glory of the world off of men and onto Jesus where it belongs. They are the words of Jesus himself as he hung upon the cross: "It is finished."

This definite and ultimate pronouncement of Jesus will resound in a myriad of situations this week as we are tempted to deviate from the gospel.

When we are tempted to try and prove ourselves to God and to others instead of recognizing our dependence on Him: It is finished.

When we look down on others because the sin we see in them reminds us of the sin we see in ourselves: It is finished.

When we are too embarrassed to own up to our own shortcomings and sin: It is finished.

And when we are tempted to hold up our scorecard of supposed righteous acts before God: It is finished.

When we re-declare the declaration of Jesus, over and over again, in situation after situation, both when we think too much of ourselves and when we think too little, we will finally begin to see the truth Paul is going to articulate as the letter to the Galatians closes in chapter 6 verse 14: "But as for me, I will never boast about anything except the cross of our Lord Jesus Christ. The world has been crucified to me through the cross, and I to the world." This is the cry of the children of God who, though they are dependent and helpless in every way, are confident in the Father who delights in providing for them.

CHAPTER 4

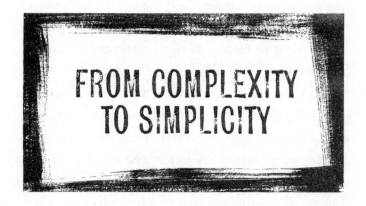

FROM COMPLEXITY
TO SIMPLICITY

"I Feel Stressed"

That's what he said. And my immediate reaction was to try and suppress a smile. But the nine-year-old up well past his bedtime standing in front of me was serious. Super-serious, as a matter of fact.

"Why are you feeling stressed, buddy?" And then my son went on to list about ten different things in his life at that moment ranging from piano lessons to the upcoming standardized testing he and his cohorts had been prepping for that were all conspiring against him.

I get it. I feel that way a lot, actually. What Joshua described as stress, I would describe as being stretched too thin. When it happens to me, I get that fluttery feeling inside my chest like I get when I have that extra cup of coffee late in the afternoon. It's when I feel completely overwhelmed at the number of different things vying for my attention and crying out to be tended to; sometimes the feeling is almost paralyzing. I know I need to eat the elephant, but I can't even figure out where to take the first bite.

It's sad to me, though, that it's already happening to my kids; sadder still is that I know it's going to get worse. But it always happens this way as you get older. You add more obligations and more responsibilities and commitments, and suddenly you turn around and wonder when everything got so complicated.

Relationships are no longer simple and honest, but are instead flooded with nonverbal signals and tainted with personal insecurity that force endless speculation of "what she really meant" even though she said something else.

Decisions are no longer straightforward "yeses" or "nos," but are instead plagued with scenario after scenario of potential consequences.

Even obedience to God seems more complex because of the feeling that you must weigh out ethical and moral issues, examining each choice from every possible angle before actually moving forward.

Yeah, Joshua—I get it. I feel it.

The Problem with Complexity

One could argue that what we're talking about here is mere busyness; it's the inability to rightly manage a calendar and properly prioritize what needs to be done on any given day. Busyness is indeed an issue that needs to be dealt with, but complexity is not so much an issue of time management as it is an issue of clutter.

You know how clutter works if you've ever had to move. You pack box after box as you start to sort through everything you've accumulated, all the while wondering why you ever thought this or that was important enough to keep. It's not that you meant to hold onto that ceramic cat from Panama City Beach or that rock you found on the really fun trip to the park—it just sort of happened. It's like you closed your eyes, and the clutter formed.

That's how complexity works, too. It happens slowly, almost imperceptibly, and over the course of time. As we start to age, clutter starts to form in our hearts and life becomes less and less simple. More and more activities, priorities, and responsibilities come your way, and suddenly you feel like a piece of leather stretched over the round base so tightly you can bounce a quarter off your heart.

It happened that way to the Israelites. The foundation of their nation started with the Ten Commandments, all of which were simple and straightforward. The Lord was very clear with his expectations, and that's when the questions started:

"Can we get some further clarification about this 'Sabbath' issue? What does it really mean to work? And while we're on the subject, we should probably propose a few amendments to this 'adultery' statement. Who exactly are we talking about here? And what technically constitutes 'adultery'?" And so on and so forth. By the time Jesus walked in Palestine, God's people had built a kind of hedge around the Mosaic law with their own verbal laws. This was to ensure that the written law was implemented in the right ways at the right times. In fact, they had codified all of the Old Testament Scriptures so that they had 613 laws. To those laws they added hundreds of rules and regulations and traditions so that in the minutest area of life the rightness or wrongness of an action was determined by a rule. For example, Exodus 31:15 lays down a rule about the seventh day of the week, reminding the people that it is to be a day dedicated to the Lord. The rabbis added a bit of complexity there as they divided work into thirty-nine categories. One specific labor forbidden was plowing on the Sabbath. But a person did not even have to use a plow to break this rule. If a person stood up from a chair and the legs made a furrow in the ground, he was accused of plowing on the Sabbath.

Though they might have begun with the best of intentions, God's people cluttered their hearts with complexity and in so doing choked out the simplicity of what it means to be his children.

The Symptoms of a Cluttered Heart

The result of complexity is a heart filled with clutter. And that clutter is manifested in a variety of ways:

- A cluttered heart lives at a hurried pace. There is no time to stop and rest because complexity constantly pulls in a thousand different directions at a time.
- A cluttered heart is only capable of superficial engagement. No real relationships of depth can be formed because there are simply too many competitors for the limited resources a single heart has to offer.
- A cluttered heart suffers from lack of focus. Complexity demands that attention and focus be constantly divided, and because they are, nothing is done with care and attention.

Worst of all, a cluttered heart squeezes out love. It makes sense, doesn't it? Because how can you have time to do something as simple as love when you are stretched so thin? Richard Foster says it like this:

Like Jack's beanstalk, our obligations seem to grow overnight. We are trapped in a rat race, not just of acquiring money, but also of meeting family and business obligations. We pant through an endless series of appointments and duties. This problem is especially acute for those who sincerely want to do what is right. With frantic fidelity we respond to all calls to service, distressingly unable to distinguish the voice of Christ from that of human manipulators. We feel bowed low with the burden of integrity.

But we do not need to be left frustrated and exhausted by the demands of life. The Christian grace of simplicity can usher us into the Center of unhurried peace and power. Like Thomas Kelly, we can come to know by experience that God "never guides us into an intolerable scramble of panting feverishness." In simplicity, we enter the deep silences of the heart for which we were created.[5]

Sounds good, doesn't it? To find true simplicity in an increasingly complex world? Imagine what it must be like to have an uncluttered heart. Imagine an undivided focus. Imagine a return to the basic truth of loving God, with all you are, and then letting that love of God spill over into love of neighbor. Imagine it; but know that no one is accidentally simple. For though a heart becomes cluttered unintentionally over time, true simplicity only comes to those who intentionally pursue it.

The same principle operates in our home. My wife is a clutter warrior. It is her weekly mission (if not daily) to wage a private war on clutter. She fights these battles with the weapons of a keen eye and an empty trash can, filling it with her spoils. Finished homework papers, completed to-do lists, unsorted random collections from our kids' adventures—these are all waiting to be plundered. The only reason our home is uncluttered is because she takes an active stance against it.

Such is the case with complexity. It can be uncluttered, but not accidentally. The child of God knows the beauty of simplicity, but only because the child of God fights for an uncluttered heart.

Focus Like a Child

Parents are liars. Come on; you know it's true. It's not that we tell outright lies to our kids; it's that we choose, on occasion, to withhold the full truth from them. We, for example, often don't let our kids in on any plan we have that's longer than a week away.

Why? For our own sanity.

Children have a laser-like focus when they see something they deem worthy of their attention. Be it a birthday party, a visit from Grandma, or even a meal at their favorite restaurant, everything else in their consciousness fades to the periphery. That's when the questions start:

- Is it Friday yet?
- Why is it taking so long to get here?
- Can we go early?
- How much time is left?

This focus, I believe, is not a bad representation of what simplicity is meant to be like in the life of the Christian. It's a single-mindedness that is rightly fixated, causing everything else to be appropriately secondary. When you have that kind of focus, life doesn't seem nearly as complex as it once did.

Jesus tells us about this kind of simplicity in Matthew 6:33: "Seek first the kingdom of God and his righteousness, and all these things will be provided for you." Simple enough. Don't seek many things; seek one thing, and watch how the rest of life is put into perspective. That's pretty clear. But what's not so clear, and yet perhaps even more descriptive, is what Jesus said just a few sentences earlier:

"The eye is the lamp of the body. If your eye is healthy, your whole body will be full of light. But if your eye is bad, your whole body will be full of darkness. So if the light within you is darkness, how deep is that darkness!" (Matt. 6:22–23)

Seems a little out of place, doesn't it? This whole section of the Sermon on the Mount is speaking against materialism and worry, since those things are often two sides of the same coin. We worry about tomorrow, so we accumulate to try and insulate ourselves against anything that could potentially harm us.

Don't be like that, says Jesus; instead of living by sight, live by faith, and trust in the God not only who can feed and clothe you but also remembers every good thing you have done and stores up future reward for you in heaven.

Then comes this thing about the eye. Strange, right? Not when you see it through the lens of simplicity. Jesus says the eye is like a lamp, and the lamp (at least in those days), wasn't just a decorative piece of extra furniture to add a splash of color to the room. The lamp was there for one reason and one reason only—illumination. And the extent of that illumination would be dependent on the quality of the lamp. Is it filled with oil? Is the glass clear or distorted? If the lamp is shaded in some way, the illumination will take on the shade of that through which it's passing.

Jesus said that the eye is the lamp of the body, and like a home needs a good lamp, so also should our eye be "good." The word translated here as "good" can also be translated as "single." If you read it again through that lens (pun intended), you get something like this:

What you have your focus on reveals the state of your heart. And there are lots of things competing for your focus, most of which can be bought with money. But you, as the children of God, need a sharp vision and single focus on one thing. When you do, the rest of everything will fade to the background.

Complexity clouds our vision. It divides our focus. But simplicity is the childlike virtue that sharpens our gaze. How do we fight for this kind of simplicity of focus? The Bible calls this fight "abiding."

The Simplicity of Abiding

Let me take you back to John 15 where Jesus told us about the imperative growth of the Christian: "I am the vine; you are the branches. Whoever abides in me and I in him, he it is that bears much fruit, for apart from me you can do nothing" (John 15:5 ESV).

In this simple verse, Jesus boils down what life in him is like: it's abiding. This is how you overcome complexity and move toward simplicity. It's not a calendar management issue; it's not a system of tasking and organization; over and above any of these tools, it is realigning your focus to be set on Jesus. This is the core of what abiding in Christ means.

Fortunately for us, the book of John doesn't only contain the command to abide in Jesus; it gives us a picture of what doing so looks like, way back in chapter one. Back then, Jesus was a relatively new figure on the religious landscape. There were rumors surrounding him—his birth, his teaching, his power—but by far, the big religious draw of the day was still John the Baptist. John, with his wild beard and locust-popping habits. John, the fearless preacher who called the Pharisees to task. John, the eccentric prophet who quoted obscure passages from centuries earlier.

But in this particular instance, John had caused a different kind of ripple. The previous day, Jesus had approached the Jordan River. John stopped what he was doing to make a mysterious but powerful declaration: "Here is the Lamb of God, who takes away the sin of the world!" (1:29). It left his disciples wondering.

Then, when the same thing happened the next day, two of those disciples wanted to inquire further:

> The next day, John was standing with two of his disciples. When he saw Jesus passing by, he said, "Look! The Lamb of God!" The two disciples heard him say this and followed Jesus. When Jesus turned and noticed them following him,

he asked them, "What are you looking for?" (John 1:35–38)

Valid question. Here were two men who were followers of John. Jesus comes walking up, and suddenly he's got two hangers-on. So what were they looking for?

Their answer seems to say, "We don't know," for at first glance they didn't even give an appropriate response. Instead of answering the question, they ask another question to Jesus: "Teacher, where are you staying?"

Another good question. It's not a good question because it redirected the question of Jesus, buying them some time to think of a better answer. It's good because of the word *staying*.

The word is the same word we find in John 15:4 (ESV), this time spoken by Jesus: "*Abide* in me, and I in you. As the branch cannot bear fruit by itself, unless it *abides* in the vine, neither can you unless you, *abide* in me."

That's what the men asked: "Where are you abiding?" Where are you remaining? Where are you dwelling? Where are you going to be, because that's where we want to go. To be with you. To remain with you. To abide with you." What we have here, then, is the answer to our own question of not only what it looks like to abide, but actually how you go about doing it.

Abiding Begins with a Glimpse of Jesus

These early disciples didn't know the ins and outs of who Jesus was; they had an inkling, but they were a long way from being able to fully understand and articulate the gospel. In their minds, the coming messiah was a political leader—maybe a general or a charismatic revolutionary who would help free the nation of Israel from Roman oppression and return them to their former glory like in the days of King David. Could this be *that* guy?

Maybe that's why they returned Jesus' question with one of their own when he asked them what they were looking for. The two guys looked at each other, shrugged their shoulders, and asked another question as if to say, "Truth is, Jesus, we don't exactly know. But we know that you're different. You're unique. And wherever you're going, we want to go there, too." This is how it begins for all of us.

We catch a glimpse of Jesus. Maybe we've got some theological background. Maybe we know better answers than these two. Or maybe we're just hearing about him for the first time. Regardless, abiding in Jesus begins not when we learn about him, but when we actually encounter him, and we find ourselves so arrested by that vision that we know we need more.

The nineteenth-century Scottish theologian Thomas Chalmers called this "the expulsive power of a new affection":

> It is seldom that any of our bad habits or flaws disappear by a mere process of natural extinction; at least it is very seldom that this is done by the instrumentality of reasoning, or by the force of mental determination. But what cannot be destroyed may be dispossessed, and one taste may be made to give way to another and to lose its power entirely as the reigning affection of the mind. The boy who ceases at length to be a slave to his appetite does so because a more mature taste has brought it into subordination. The young man may cease to idolize sensual pleasure, but it is because the idol of wealth has gotten the ascendancy, so the love of money can cast out the love of sloth. However, even the love of money can cease to have mastery over the heart if it is drawn into the world of ideology and politics and he is now lorded over by a love of power and moral superiority. But there is not one of these transformations in which the heart is left without an object. The heart's desire for an ultimate object may be conquered, but its desire to have SOME object is unconquerable.

The only way to dispossess the heart of an old affection is through the expulsive power of a new one.[6]

To put it in more contemporary terms, a person might spend their entire childhood eating cheeseburgers from Burger King. Eventually, though, they might decide due to an expanding waistline and heightening cholesterol count to cut back. The question, though, is what is going to take the place of their former affection. According to Chalmers, there must be something. And unless that "something" is of greater satisfaction than what is abandoned, it's only a matter of time until that guy finds himself in the drive-through lane once again.

To truly abide in Christ, we must start with a glimpse of Christ. And in that glimpse of him we will find the only true power that can hold our attention and focus for an eternity—the Son of God himself. Once our imagination and love are captured, life starts becoming less and less complex.

Thing is, though, we don't have to sit around and wait for that to happen; these early disciples didn't. Though abiding begins with a glimpse of Jesus, it continues with an intentional choice.

Abiding Is an Intentional Choice

I don't spend a lot of time on boats, but whenever I do, I am always a little bit amazed at the power of the current in the water. It's one of those forces that's always there, no matter how still and pristine a body of water might seem, still churning and moving below the surface.

Imagine with me that you go out on a boat on one of those clear, warm early summer days. The clouds are minimal, and the wind is even less, so you cruise out to the middle of the lake on what seems like a sheet of glass. You can shut down the motor of the boat right in the middle with the intent of letting the kids swim for a while. And, for the next hour or so you throw each other off the boat, practice cannonballs, and have a snack. But then, inevitably, you have to restart and reposition the boat, because even though you turned off the motor in the middle, you look up and notice that you are closer to one side of shore than you were an hour before.

Why? It's because you've drifted. You didn't mean to move; you had no intention of changing your position. You just stopped fighting the current; you stopped paying attention. Because there are constant currents, you are always moving—whether you recognize it or not. When you're out on the lake, unless you choose to take an active effort against doing so, you are going to drift.

That's actually true in all areas of life. Drifting is bound to happen without intentionality:

- You might mean to cut down on your spending this year, but without intentionality, you are going to drift from that vision.
- You might want to eat less sugar this year, but unless you pay attention, you will drift from your goals.
- You might intend to read more and watch TV less, but unless you take active measures to do so, you will drift.

When you do nothing, you drift, and you drift despite all the good intentions, grandiose claims, and resolute statements. You are always going to drift. And you know what else? No one drifts toward Jesus.

No one ever did nothing and woke up closer to Jesus the next day than they were before. We drift away from him, not toward. If we want to move toward Jesus, it's going to take an active stance against the current that's always moving us further and further out.

That's why the writer of Hebrews tells us to do something very simple and yet very profound at the same time: "We must pay attention all the more to what we have heard, so that we will not drift away" (Heb. 2:1). Pay attention, because if you're not paying active attention, you are going to drift. And if you drift, it's always going to be away from Jesus, not toward him. These men in John 1 made an intentional choice of focus. Even though they didn't know what they were looking for precisely, they chose to go and be with him.

The simplicity of abiding in Christ isn't going to happen by accident. Today, like every day, we will have to bring some intentionality to our Christian walk. We aren't going to stumble into abiding; we've got to make the intentional choice to meet Jesus where he is. We've got to open the Bible. We've got to pray. We've got to reflect. And in each case, and on each day, we've got to choose to do it over and over again. As life becomes more and more complex, we must make intentional choices about where we want to focus ourselves. If we do nothing at all, our natural course is to drift further from Jesus rather than toward him.

Abiding Is Driven by Faith

Sometimes the faith is small, but in each case, we catch a glimpse of Jesus. We make an intentional choice to be with him. And then we find ourselves choosing to do so again and again out of faith.

Let's not make the mistake of thinking that abiding in Jesus is purely an act of the will; it's not. It's driven forward by faith. There will be times when you don't feel like abiding. You're too tired. You have too much to do. Something else seems more important. What we must do in those times is more than act; we must believe. We must believe that Jesus, no matter how much we want to abide with him, actually wants to abide with us even more. This faith works itself out in all kinds of everyday, practical ways:

- We believe the Bible is God's Word, so we take action on that belief and set the alarm clock for thirty minutes earlier.
- We believe that treasure in heaven is better than treasure on earth, so we take action on that belief and form a budget we can live generously inside of.
- We believe that the kingdom is of primary and utmost importance, so we take action on that belief and fix our eyes on Jesus singularly and let the other priorities of life be framed with our vision of him.

Abiding becomes more than an idea or an aspiration; it's a state of simplicity that we fight daily for. When we do, we find a funny thing happening.

Back in John 1, there's one other detail that lets us know what the experience of abiding is like. John records the actual time these disciples followed Jesus—about ten a.m.—but then also tells us that they stayed with him all day (John 1:39). He drops this in as if to say, "And can you believe it? When we looked up, the whole day was gone!"

That's simplicity. That's focus. That's childlike. Rather than checking for messages on the iPhone or worrying about what has to come next, these men were lost in the power of a new affection. Suddenly, like children, all of the other aspects of life that were crowding around them suddenly didn't seem that important. Complexity was reduced to simplicity in the presence of Jesus.

CHAPTER 5

The Pool Incident

Children are public people. If you've spent a lot of time around children, you'll know that's true, because chances are they've told you about everything from their favorite games to play to what bodily function they think is the funniest at a given moment.

I remember a time, when my kids were much smaller and we were enjoying an afternoon at the local YMCA swimming pool. (I say "enjoying" here, even though to me one of the greatest parts about having teenagers is that I will never have to visit a public pool again. Because, after all, who doesn't love walking around half dressed in front of strangers in the sweltering heat?) At that time, we still had kiddos wearing swim diapers, which are basically a toddler version of a straitjacket. These things are impossible to remove, especially when they're wet. They are, nonetheless, a necessary evil to avoid the dreaded "pool accident."

An hour into the pool time, and you guessed it— the little Kelley kid wearing the swim diaper needed to go to the bathroom. Now if there is something worse than a swim diaper at the YMCA in the middle of July, it certainly is going to the fungus-infested public bathroom and trying to remove said swim diaper at the YMCA. At the moment the call for the potty came, this dad just didn't have it in him.

"Are you sure you can't wait for a little while?"

He couldn't. He had to go right then, and so I did what I'm sure (hope?) many other dads would have done in the same position, facing the task of navigating that swim diaper in the bathroom. I told him to go in the pool.

"No, Daddy. We don't do that."

"I know we don't, buddy, but just this once it will be okay."

"Are you sure?"

"Yes. I'm sure."

This is the point in the story where I became distracted by one of the other kids wanting to show me their latest pool trick, and so I temporarily diverted my attention from my full-bladdered son. Imagine my pride when a millisecond later I turned back around to find that same boy, not only standing on the edge of the pool, but apparently having had no trouble negotiating the swim diaper on his own. For there he stood, in all his glory, swim diaper to the knees, doing his business. In the pool. Off the side.

See? No sense of privacy. And while that complete transparency is beguiling to parents, it's also part of the beautiful innocence of childhood. No child wonders whether he or she will be judged by those around him; no child thinks about being made fun of if they reveal something about themselves; no child considers that others might not be particularly interested in what is most interesting to them at a given moment.

They just are. And they are what they are what they are.

As we grow up, though, we gravitate more and more toward a greater and greater need for privacy. While that sense of privacy is appropriate in many cases, it must be held in tension with the fact that we were created to live in open community with each other as the children of God. If indeed we are going to grow up in Christ, then we must grow down in this over-inflated desire for privacy, exchanging it for the kind of open and genuine transparency that comes when we know we are fully and truly accepted through Jesus. When we, as God's children, are convinced of this, we will be free to both fully love and be loved by others.

The Theology of "Us"

If you go back to the beginning, and I mean the very beginning, you find that the universe was created for the pleasure of and at the spoken command of God. There was nothing—and then there was . . . everything. With a word spoken into the formless void, stars, planets, animals, plants, and everything else right down to the molecular level came into being. God did this. God alone could.

In reading the account in Genesis 1, you find that as this good work of systematically creating all we know was accomplished, the same refrain appears after each act: God saw that it was good.

And, of course, it was. Everything was right. All was in harmony. Every atom and every particle placed in its divinely orchestrated position, all culminating with the creation of the first man, uniquely created in God's own image, placed in the perfect garden.

But it's at this point the refrain falters (if indeed such a thing can be said). For while everything was good, there was one thing that was not: "It is not good for the man to be alone" (Gen. 2:18). Thus sayeth the Lord.

But soon he was not alone. The Lord fashioned the perfect complement, of like kind, for his first man. The same statement is as true for us today as it was for Adam then: "It is not good for the man to be alone."

God created this man in his image, which entails the unique need, desire, and capacity for relationship. We were meant to be together, both with each other and with God. It is no accident that in that garden, free from the perversion of sin, this first man and woman were naked and felt no shame. They hid nothing from each other or from God but were instead laid bare in all ways. But the genuine harmony of those first days was not to last.

Fear and Shame in the Garden

Born from the lips of the lying serpent, this man and woman believed a great and terrible lie about God. Though couched in terms more pleasing to the ear, the snake leveled a charge against the character of God. The lie behind the words was that God did not really love them, and that he was surely holding out on them. And the man and woman believed.

As a result came the first experience of two things that still plague our lives today: fear and shame.

"I heard you in the garden, and I was afraid because I was naked, so I hid" (Gen. 3:10). Here we remain. The difference is that now we hide behind cleverly posed and worded social media posts and we clothe ourselves with pleasant platitudes. The setting and the attempts might change, but we are still there, aren't we? Cowering in the trees. Suddenly aware of our own vulnerability.

This sense of vulnerability is, ironically, also part of getting older. Once upon a time, as children, we not only lived out in the open in full view of everyone else; we also lived with a sense of immortality. Nothing seemed too dangerous, and we didn't believe that we could actually be hurt in either an emotional or physical way. So we lived with abandon, unapologetic for our adventures or our self-confession. But the years have taught us differently. We have a long list of broken bones, stitches, and wounded hearts that show us just how vulnerable we really are. That's why we find ourselves in the trees; we feel the need, as adults, to protect ourselves from anyone and anything that might do us harm.

We spend an incredible amount of time and energy maintaining our precious privacy, all rooted in the fear and shame that all of us bear in one way or another. We are afraid of what would happen if we were truly laid bare before another and are ashamed of what that other might see if they truly saw us at all.

The Fear of Being Found Out

"Is today going to be the day?"

At some level, I believe most of us live with this question. It's the question of being found out.

By "found out," I don't mean that some secret sin we've been treasuring will be brought into the open. It's bigger than that. It's the same sensation Adam and Eve were coping with in the garden with their feeble attempts to cover their own nakedness. Most of us are walking through life in various degrees and in various situations in which we feel radically unequipped and unbelievably unqualified. With that in mind, the question might start to sound like this:

"Is today going to be the day my boss finds out I actually don't know how to run this project?"

"Is today going to be the day my kids find out I don't really know how to parent teenagers?"

"Is today going to be the day that my friends discover I'm not actually as clever as they might think?"

It's paralyzing, this fear of being found out. Of being discovered to be somehow "less" than the perception that others have of you. It's the feeling of wondering whether or not the next action, the next tweet, the next post, the next statement, is going to be funny enough, smart enough, penetrating enough, clever enough to buy us just a little more time. And if we're not careful, we can find ourselves devoting endless energy to making sure that carefully crafted persona continues to withstand any scrutiny that comes its way. We can drift into lies, disingenuous actions, and running in fear, all because of what might happen if we are actually found out. So it seems that we actually have not come that far from those days in the garden when the first man and the first woman hid in their own fear and shame.

The remedy for our own fear and shame is the same one God provided for Adam and Eve—the gospel. It's in that same garden, now marred by sin, that we find the first shadows of the remedy for sin and all the fear and shame that comes along with it: "I will put hostility between you and the woman, and between your offspring and her offspring. He will strike your head, and you will strike his heel" (Gen. 3:15). "The LORD God made clothing from skins for the man and his wife, and he clothed them" (Gen. 3:21).

The Son of Man will crush the serpent's head. And because of Jesus' work, we as the children of God through faith in the gospel, are clothed with something far better than animal skins. We are clothed with the righteousness of Christ. It is through the gospel that we can return to that glorious innocence that children so naturally possess, where hiding is only the stuff of games and shame is never even in the back of our minds.

The gospel is the battering ram for fear and shame. But fear and shame aren't broken down by inflating our egos. The gospel does not lie to us and tell us that we are indeed as clever or as qualified or as wise or as engaging as we might appear. In fact, it's just the opposite.

The gospel reminds us that not only are we not everything people think we are; we are actually much, much worse. There is more darkness, more bitterness, more hatred, more jealousy, and more laziness lurking within our souls than we would even admit to ourselves. And yet Jesus has died and risen again to forgive and redeem that very darkness. The gospel, then, drives out our fear of being found out, not by telling us we're not that bad, but instead by reminding us that from God's perspective, there is truly nothing left to find out. He has mined every corner and explored every crevice of our hearts. He knows it all, and yet Jesus willingly gave himself for our sake.

The sweet freedom from the exhausting fear of being found out happens when we encounter the message that God fully knows us, even more than we know ourselves, and died for us anyway. The result is that we can finally come out from behind the trees. We are, like children, free to know and be known, free to be fully loved and to fully love others in return. The incubator where this kind of freedom is grown and developed is the church.

"Share"

The church is where we move from privacy to authenticity. It only makes sense why that would be so, since the communion of the saints should be where everyone is most cognizant of their own sin. If indeed what unites is the gospel, and in believing the gospel is an inherent recognition of our own wicked hopelessness before God, then here of all places is where we have nothing to lose.

The ground is level at the foot of the cross, and all of us are standing there together. There is no room in that posture of abject need to put on airs or false faces. Ironic, then, that the church is often where we feel compelled to be the most pridefully private.

Unspoken prayer requests, "fine, just fine," and "bless your hearts" abound. But when we operate at this kind of surface level relationship with the rest of God's church, we are robbing ourselves of one of God's greatest gifts to us—the gift of each other. The Bible shows us how precious this gift can be when we are willing to drop the coating of privacy and live freely with one another, as we see happening with the early church in Acts 2:44–47:

Now all the believers were together and held all things in common. They sold their possessions and property and distributed the proceeds to all, as any had need. Every day they devoted themselves to meeting together in the temple, and broke bread from house to house. They ate their food with joyful and sincere hearts, praising God and enjoying the favor of all the people. Every day the Lord added to their number those who were being saved.

These early believers knew what it meant to "share." They shared everything, from their needs to their fears to their faith to their possessions. We, also, like to share, and thanks to technology, it is easier to "share" than ever before. But now, "sharing" is about posting. It's about photos, videos, statuses, blog posts, and whatever else we dump onto the social media machine. Every crafted photo, every captured moment, every clever statement or hot take on the current issue we have is now "sharable." And we measure the value of those photos, moments, and statements based on how many subsequent times they are liked and re-shared.

Technology has not only enabled us to share more from a volume standpoint; it has also enabled us to share higher quality things. Thanks to filters, the ease of picture-taking, and quick editing, you can make sure that every image is rightly lit and perfectly posed and that every statement has just the right amount of snark and cleverness. These are our best moments, our best statements, and our best thoughts, "shared."

I personally don't have a problem with that. In the old days, when you would invite someone over to look at your vacation slide show, you wouldn't include the pictures that "didn't make the cut." So in this very public forum, there is a certain amount of discretion that is rightly applied when we choose not to dump all our dirty laundry all over the Internet. But this new version of "sharing," in which we share in both great quantity and quality, has to be amended when it comes to the church. For in the church, we have a very simple and yet increasingly difficult-to-follow command found in Romans 12:9–15:

> Let love be without hypocrisy. Detest evil; cling to what is good. Love one another deeply as brothers and sisters. Outdo one another in showing honor. Do not lack diligence in zeal; be fervent in the Spirit; serve the Lord. Rejoice in hope; be patient in affliction; be persistent in prayer. Share with the saints in their needs; pursue hospitality. Bless those who persecute you; bless and do not curse. Rejoice with those who rejoice; weep with those who weep.

These are some of the very practical applications of the very thorough explanation of the gospel Paul had given in the first eleven chapters of Romans. But these commands are mostly all "one another" in nature, meaning they cannot be obeyed apart from our relationships with each other. In particular, though, notice the very last sentence of the passage:

"Rejoice with those who rejoice; weep with those who weep." (v. 15)

In the church, we cannot weep with each other if we never see or know that we are weeping. And here's where we find the rub with our "sharing." In our new day of "sharing," we are liberal with our triumphs but greedy with our pain. And while that might pass just fine on Facebook, it will not do in the church.

"I'm a private person," we might argue. "It's no one else's business," we might say. "It's my cross to bear," we might conclude. And yet we still find these challenging words for the church: Weep with those who weep.

As the people of God, we have a communal responsibility for each other. To live in obedience to that vision of the church, we must be willing to share—but not just share the best of us. We cannot hoard our pain and weakness, but must, in a more genuine and authentic way than ever before, disclose ourselves to each other. And then we will truly not only "like" each other, but weep with each other.

Butting up against this command from Scripture is our pride. It's ironic how closely fear, shame, and pride walk together in our lives. We are held in bondage by fear and shame, and it is pride that keeps us from actually coming out from behind the trees and living in true relationship with each other. Once again, it is the gospel that allows us to come out into the open. The gospel helps us come from behind the trees because we no longer have to prove anything to anyone, for Jesus has fully justified us at the cross. And the gospel allows us to bear the burdens of someone else because we no longer feel threatened by someone else's joys and successes. Jesus has freed us to actually be—to be happy, to be sad, to be excited, and ultimately to be ourselves without holding anything back. This is part of the glorious freedom of God's children—it's knowing that we don't have anything left to prove to anyone else.

This is, of course, great in concept. I mean, who doesn't resonate with the idea of living without feeling like you have to hold something back? Who doesn't love the vision of life where you're not constantly afraid of being found out? But in practice? It's one thing to talk about the benefits of coming out from behind those trees in the garden; it's a different matter to actually do it. Frankly, this level of genuine authenticity is too much for most adults to take. It's far safer when we retreat inside ourselves and only display a false version of ourselves just as we often do online. So how does this begin to happen in practice?

Let me offer one simple suggestion about how we begin to grow down in privacy and grow up in authenticity in the church—it's by recovering the Christian discipline of hospitality.

The Remedy of Hospitality

Hospitality was an important quality that characterized the New Testament church, one that the biblical writers saw the vital importance of:

- "Be hospitable to one another without complaining" (1 Pet. 4:9).
- "Share with the saints in their needs; pursue hospitality" (Rom. 12:13).
- "Don't neglect to show hospitality, for by doing this some have welcomed angels as guests without knowing it" (Heb. 13:2).

I personally struggle with that in relation to some other characteristics the Bible tells us to pursue. Patience? I get it. Love? Sure. Hope? Joy? Absolutely. But hospitality is a struggle for me precisely because I have an overdeveloped sense of privacy. Like most other adults, I like my personal space, my personal thoughts, and my personal time. The very nature of hospitality requires me to share what I consider to be "personal" with others in a sacrificial way. True enough, there are some who gravitate more naturally toward this kind of sharing with others; they are bent toward a more "public" approach to life than others.

I live with someone like this. My sweet wife, on a near weekly basis, is welcoming someone into our home, making something delicious to eat, or giving of her time to sit with someone and listen. But if you take the words of Scripture seriously, hospitality is more than a character trait that is easier for some than others to practice; it's a command. Hospitality is to be pursued, and not neglected, without complaining.

And here is where the temptation comes in for me—and perhaps for all introverted folks out there. We tend to think of hospitality as a single action that is pursued occasionally, as if we are on some kind of a quota system. I, and maybe you, think that if we do something hospitable every once in a while, we can check off the box for the month and feel free to go back to our private lives until we feel some measure of guilt again.

But for the Christian, hospitality is not just an act to be performed; it is a posture to be assumed. Furthermore, it's through the intentional recovery of this discipline that we will find ourselves more able to live in authenticity.

To understand why that is, we need first to understand what hospitality really is. While there are certain acts, like making the casserole or opening your home, that are indicative of hospitality, the characteristic itself has a deeper meaning and implication than these actions. The word *hospitality* comes from the combination of two words: "love" and "stranger." Literally, then, hospitality is the love of strangers.

This is a powerful description of what the gospel is. When we were strangers and aliens, God took us in. When we were without a home and family, God brought us into his. When we were without hope in the world, God adopted us as his children. In the ultimate act of hospitality, God provided a way to welcome us through the death of Jesus Christ. God is ultimately hospitable, and therefore, hospitality is a characteristic built into the spiritual DNA of all those who have experienced this divine hospitality.

Hospitality, then, is the characteristic that compels us to put aside our own interests, to lay down our own desires, and to welcome the needs of others ahead of our own, just as Jesus did with his life and death, and just as we are told to do:

> If then there is any encouragement in Christ, if any consolation of love, if any fellowship with

the Spirit, if any affection and mercy, make my
joy complete by thinking the same way, having
the same love, united in spirit, intent on one
purpose. Do nothing out of selfish ambition or
conceit, but in humility consider others as more
important than yourselves. Everyone should
look out not only for his own interests, but also
for the interests of others. (Phil. 2:1–4)

Jesus, during his life, epitomized hospitality, even
though he had no home. Even though he did not have
physical resources. Even though he didn't have an oven
or a cookie sheet or a casserole dish. Jesus practiced
the core of hospitality, which is sacrificing something
of your own to welcome others in. That thing might be
your privacy, but it might also involve your time, your
resources, or your emotional investment. At its core,
hospitality is welcoming others in so that their needs
might be met at the expense of your own. This is why
hospitality is not merely a set of actions; it's a posture
of living.

Why does the intentional practice of hospitality
lead us to grow up in authenticity? It's because when
we welcome others into our lives, we find ourselves
increasingly in the habit of sharing life with them as
well. Through hospitality in its various forms, the
body of Christ demonstrates that we are welcoming to
each other, willing to bear one another's burdens. We

find ourselves increasingly operating in the freedom of authenticity that is so natural to children, but so difficult for adults.

Our insatiable need for privacy is, in large part, just a mask for the fear and shame that still bind us. But as the children of God, we can come out from behind the trees. We can find a God there who has clothed us in a better way than we could ever clothe ourselves. And we will also find others, who, like us, have been covered with the righteousness of Christ. There, standing in the freedom of intimacy, we can finally be genuine with one another, not because we have nothing to hide, but because God has seen everything we have to hide. And he loves us anyway.

CHAPTER 6

Tornado Warning

I'm a bit of a weather nerd. If you ask my wife, that last sentence is an understatement; she gets no end of enjoyment watching me stand on the porch, simultaneously watching the clouds and the weather app on my phone. But unlike the typical weather nerd, I'm not standing on that porch in the blinding rain out of fascination or enjoyment; I'm standing there out of anxiety.

I grew up in the Panhandle of Texas, right around the dumpster of Tornado Alley. In the spring and early summer, we would have two to three tornado warnings a week, and I would wake up on a near daily basis and turn on the weather just to see if I had anything to worry about that day. That anxiety has stayed with me these thirty or so years, and though I do have a "wake me up" app on my phone just in case of a funnel cloud, I still live with that general sense of worry when I know a storm is coming.

My kids do not.

I've often wondered why not. It might be that they haven't been around enough tornadoes. Or it might be they haven't seen the cinematic masterpiece that is *Twister*. Or it might be that they really, deep in their hearts, actually do want to go to Oz. I think, though, their lack of anxiety is really, in a strange way, a compliment to my own anxiety. They know that Dad is on the porch, and that Dad has his clever app, and that Dad knows when we need to go to the basement. They don't worry because they know me.

Or at least they think they do. See, they are still young enough to believe that I can actually keep them safe in all circumstances. They haven't aged into the realization that I am radically out of control, and that despite my best efforts, bad things are going to happen. I'm not a kid anymore, though, and because I'm not, I get it. I get that I can't control the weather. Furthermore, I've had just enough life experience to know that my anxiety is warranted. In fact, I suppose the only way that I could be relieved of anxiety is if I knew there was another person standing on the porch with me who could do things like control when storms start and stop. If that were true, my worry would be misplaced. Even foolish. In that case, I would actually have an even more grounded kind of trust than that which my own children put in me, for my faith would be not only in one who wants the best for me, but one who could actually make it happen.

The Capacity for Worry

There are plenty of things in the world to worry about. In fact, as I've grown further into adulthood, I've almost daily found more and more reasons for anxiety. There might be, then, no more countercultural command than the one we find from Jesus in the Sermon on the Mount:

> "Don't worry about your life, what you will eat or what you will drink; or about your body, what you will wear. Isn't life more than food and the body more than clothing? Consider the birds of the sky: They don't sow or reap or gather into barns, yet your heavenly Father feeds them. Aren't you worth more than they? Can any of you add one moment to his life-span by worrying? And why do you worry about clothes? Observe how the wildflowers of the field grow:

They don't labor or spin thread. Yet I tell you that not even Solomon in all his splendor was adorned like one of these. If that's how God clothes the grass of the field, which is here today and thrown into the furnace tomorrow, won't he do much more for you—you of little faith? So don't worry, saying, 'What will we eat?' or 'What will we drink?' or 'What will we wear?' For the Gentiles eagerly seek all these things, and your heavenly Father knows that you need them." (Matt. 6:25–32)

Make no mistake—the issue of worry, to Jesus, is not merely emotional. And his command in this passage carries with it the same weight as any of his other commands in Scripture. We make a drastic error when we think that this command regarding worry is in a different category than his commands regarding adultery, lying, or anything else. The Son of God, with all the authority of heaven, says that the children of God must not worry. That means the anxiety I feel is more than a momentary feeling; it's outright disobedience to Jesus.

This is where I take a bit of offense, because frankly, as an adult, the command to not worry seems a bit unrealistic. *Don't worry? Come on, Jesus. You can't really mean that. I mean, look at the level of responsibility I have. And have you looked around the world lately? Imagine trying to raise a kid in these circumstances.*

It's a nice idea and all, but it's really not practical. The very suggestion that we should not worry is not only a denial of reality; it's actually irresponsible. But when we think more deeply about the issue of worry and anxiety, we come to see that worry is really a barometer of what we believe about God. And now we're back to the subject of weather.

A barometer is an instrument used to measure atmospheric pressure. Why would we want to measure atmospheric pressure? Certainly not for the fascination of doing so. Atmospheric pressure is really just a checkpoint to help predict short-term changes in weather. As the atmospheric pressure changes, the actual weather conditions are sure to follow. A barometer, then, is an instrument that gives a good indicator of something else—something much more relevant and important. Such is worry to the life of the Christian.

Worry is more than a negative character trait or a habit to overcome. Worry is a barometer that reveals what we believe to be true—or not true—about God at the deepest levels of our souls.

Powerful, Loving, and Wise

If it's true that worry is revelatory of what we believe, or don't believe, to be true about God, then finding ourselves in the grip of anxiety reveals that

something has short-circuited in our understanding of
who God is. Even more specifically, our anxiety reveals
that we have begun to believe that God is not powerful,
that he is not loving, or that he is not wise.

You would think that believing God is powerful
should be a given, and yet our level of anxiety might
reveal that we are only giving lip service to the supposed power of God. We might remember the teaching pictures from Sunday school where God threw the
stars into the sky and breathed out the alligator and the
zebra; we might know by heart how he parted the Red
Sea so his people could walk across on dry land; we
might recite from memory the story of how he burned
up Elijah's altar though it was soaked with water; but
our own life experiences often fail to measure up to
those grand displays of power. As we have aged into
adulthood, all those stories became just that to us—
stories—and we are left hoping against hope that God
truly is powerful after all, though we don't see any real
evidence in our own experience.

Or perhaps we do believe God is powerful, but we
don't really believe he is loving. Not really. Because as
we've gotten older, we have had one too many experiences with what love is supposed to be like. Those
experiences have taught us that love is a passing affection, here today and gone tomorrow. Or that love
means using someone else for your own gratification

and ends. Or that love is only applicable when times are convenient. All in all, we are burned out on love. It would be great if there were some God up there in the cosmic heavens who did love us, but we can't seem to muster up the emotional energy to believe it could be so. Not again.

Or perhaps we don't struggle to believe that God is powerful, and we do not even doubt that he is loving. Maybe our issue is with his wisdom. We have serious doubts about whether God knows the right time to exercise all this power and love that we believe he has. If that's true, God becomes little more than a child himself. He is a bit like Richie Rich—a child who has all the affection and all the power he could ever ask for, and yet lacks the street smarts to know the right time and place for it to be exercised. God, in that scenario, comes off as a socially awkward deity, one who embarrasses you with his level of inappropriate affection and can't seem to get out of the way of his own power.

We are anxious people because we have stopped believing in one of these three things. Unlike children who implicitly and innocently trust that their parents know, are able, and are willing to do what is best for them, we have lived just enough life to wonder if that's true of our heavenly Father. So what's the way back? How do we grow back down, having grown up so much?

What If . . .

My now six-year-old was once upon a time scared of "monsters." Monsters in the bed, under the bed, on the side of the bed—occasionally monsters in the closet. So I, as a dad, became the monster-seeker. I would go to his room at night, showing him all sides of the bed, assuring him that there were actually no monsters around. And, every once in a while, my assurance that the monsters weren't real actually did indeed drive out the fear and enable him to sleep well.

We might argue the same thing is true when it comes to our grown-up anxiety and worry. The saying goes that 90 percent of the things I worry about never really happen, and so the solution to my anxiety is to beat it back by telling myself, "Those monsters aren't real."

The problem is the 10 percent. Those monsters of job loss? Of economic downturn? Of disease? Of relational strife? Of whatever? These are real. That 10 percent is all too real, and it's coming for you. If not now, then soon. Ten percent of tragedy. Ten percent of pain. Ten percent of difficulty.

Now we are told "there is no fear in love; instead, perfect love drives out fear," in 1 John 4:18, but how does that work? What does this perfect love of God say as it drives out fear of what might be? It's not by convincing us that our worries aren't valid because those things we worry about aren't going to happen; the Lord is not so condescending as to offer us a trite, "Don't worry about that. That's silly."

Instead, the perfect love of God, when confronted with all our anxiety, worry, and fear—all our "what ifs"—replies, "What if it does?"

What if the business fails?

What if the disease comes?

What if the economy crumbles?

And the love of God says, "What if it does?"

Would any of those things separate us from the love and presence of Jesus? Would any of these occurrences, bad though they may be, truly call into question the eternal security stored up for us? Would that change the character of a good, loving, and powerful God?

What if it does?

Fear is driven out by the love of God. Not because that 10 percent won't happen, but because even when it does, it does not change the demonstrated love of God—not one iota. Unfortunately, we find ourselves most of the time looking at the wrong thing, and our misplaced gaze only serves to further our building anxiety.

Lyin' Eyes

Our eyes are one of the primary ways by which we process reality. It is through our eyes that we see the world, and it's through our eyes that we begin first to interpret and process what's happening in our lives. Sounds simple enough . . . if you can trust your eyes. But sometimes we can't.

I remember when I was a kid, my family and pretty much all my friends were drawn into the fad of the 3D holographic prints. You might remember these things—maybe you also were a victim of the cruel joke where everyone unfocuses their eyes, stares blankly at a repeating pattern, and then in awe and wonder *claim* they see a different image suddenly popping out at them.

I never saw it. I remain convinced that they're all in on an elaborate hoax.

"It's a rocket!"

"It's a grasshopper!"

"It's a panda bear!"

It's hogwash. Or at least that's what I told myself. Though it became a big joke around my house at the time, the truth was I was a little unnerved in thinking that there really was something there, but my eyes, for whatever reason, just couldn't see it. The reason this was concerning to me was that I didn't like the idea that I couldn't trust my own eyes. That there was some reality right in front of me that for whatever reason I was unable to see. That, to put a fine point on it, my eyes were lying to me.

As disconcerting as that thought may be, that's exactly what the Bible tells us is reality. We think we can trust the information provided to us by our senses, particularly our eyes, and yet God's Word lets us know that there are at least two ways our eyes can deceive us.

First of all, our eyes tell us we are too small. I think of the story of God's people, freshly and miraculously delivered from their servitude in Egypt, marching toward God's Promised Land for them. This had been a very long time in coming—generations since God first made this promise to their father Abraham. But upon returning from scouting out the land God had already promised was theirs, ten of the twelve spies were troubled:

> "We can't attack the people because they are stronger than we are!" So they gave a negative report to the Israelites about the land they had scouted: "The land we passed through to explore is one that devours its inhabitants, and all the people we saw in it are men of great size. We even saw the Nephilim there—the descendants of Anak come from the Nephilim! To ourselves we seemed like grasshoppers, and we must have seemed the same to them." (Num. 13:31–33)

The deceptive eyes of the ten spies told them they were the size of grasshoppers, and therefore didn't stand a chance against the giant inhabitants of the land. And so, despite the promises of God that compelled them forward, they convinced the people to go backward, and they languished in the wilderness for it.

Now this is not the kind of thing where we can take Scripture and interpret it to say, "God wants health, wealth, and prosperity for you! Just get up and take it!" But it is the kind of thing where we can look to the promises God has made in his Word—that he is for us, that he will complete his work in us, that he will give us our daily bread, that his grace is never in short supply—and be confident in his power to do what he said. In many of those cases, our eyes will tell us otherwise. It is not, to be specific, that we are actually greater or bigger or more courageous or more whatever than our eyes tell us, but that God's promises defy the physical circumstances that might lie before us. The promises of God prove our eyes to be liars.

But sometimes our eyes lie to us, not in telling us that we are too small, but in telling us we are too big. There is a warning from the book of Proverbs that goes like this:

> Trust in the LORD with all your heart, and do not lean on your own understanding. In all your ways acknowledge him, and he will make straight your paths. Be not wise in your own

eyes; fear the LORD, and turn away from evil. (Prov. 3:5–7 ESV)

Our eyes might tell us that we have life figured out. That we understand the nature of the universe, and even the depths of our own sinfulness, to the extent that we can captain our own ship. This is more than an overestimation of ourselves; it is idolatry and "self-lordship." And yet it is such an easy pathway to begin to walk down.

It starts out innocently enough—things in life are rolling along relatively smoothly, our decisions seem to be the right ones, and so we continue to press onward. But slowly we become convinced that we are incapable of making a mistake, that our motives are what we think they are, and that we cannot possibly be suffering under the spell of self-deception. We are then way too big, and our eyes have deceived us again.

So our eyes might convince us we are too small; our eyes might convince us we are too big. What is the solution to these eyes of ours that can be so deceptive? It's the same answer for our anxiety. To take our gaze off of ourselves, our circumstances, and whatever else might be causing us to worry, and recast our gaze on Jesus:

> Therefore, since we also have such a large cloud of witnesses surrounding us, let us lay aside every hindrance and the sin that so easily

ensnares us. Let us run with endurance the race that lies before us, keeping our eyes on Jesus, the source and perfecter of our faith. For the joy that lay before him, he endured the cross, despising the shame, and sat down at the right hand of the throne of God. (Heb. 12:1–2)

When our gaze is fixed on Jesus, we find that we are not actually living by sight at all, but rather by faith. Our hearts gaze unflinchingly upon him, and we continue the race with confidence, knowing that while our eyes might deceive us, the author and finisher of our faith never will. If we want to return to the childlike faith that is the true antidote for worry, the pathway is through looking to Jesus again and again, and more particularly to the cross. For it's at the cross that we see the display of God's power, love, and wisdom all in six terrible and glorious hours.

God's Demonstration

The cross is a grand intersection—the cosmic hinge that not only saves sinners, but also proves once and for all who God is. It's at the cross where we find the demonstration of those three qualities—God's love, his power, and his wisdom—and it's therefore at the cross where we find the true antidote for our anxiety. This is why Paul adamantly stated that God not only professes his love for his people, but actually demonstrates it at Calvary: "But God proves his own love for us in that while we were still sinners, Christ died for us" (Rom. 5:8).

The death of Jesus is the historical proof of God's love. God not only said he loved us; he demonstrated it once and for all at the cross so that one might never again call into legitimate question whether or not God is for us.

But the cross does more than show us God's love; it also shows us God's power. This might seem counter-intuitive at first, for if God were indeed so powerful, surely he would act with all the resources at his disposal to prevent something as tragic as the murder of his own Son. True enough, one might look to the cross and see a God of great weakness. But there is another perspective that we find in Scripture that demonstrates not a God incapable of intervening, but one who is in fact intervening in the most eternal way imaginable. This is what Paul is getting at in the thesis statement of the book of Romans: "For I am not ashamed of the gospel, because it is the power of God for salvation to everyone who believes, first to the Jew, and also to the Greek" (Rom. 1:16).

In the crucifixion, God displayed his great power and might by accomplishing what no human could ever do on their own. He accomplished righteousness for all who believe, past, present, and future. Why does this require so much power? We can only understand it when we begin to understand that sin is so heinous.

One of the reasons we fail to grasp the gravity of the cross is because, once again, we have such an inflated estimation of ourselves. We refuse, in our sin, to consider ourselves to be "that bad," and as soon as we begin to treat sin like a simple mistake or a lapse in judgment, we by proxy begin to devalue what God accomplished at the cross.

If, however, we come to glimpse the pure, white-hot holiness of God, and then see the undiluted evil of our sin in its light, we can start to testify in wonder at the power of God at the cross. What power is this indeed whereby a perfect God could not simply pass over our sin and thereby compromise His own perfect justice, but instead, make us righteous so that we can be with him forever? "For the word of the cross is foolishness to those who are perishing, but it is the power of God to us who are being saved" (1 Cor. 1:18).

The cross, then, reveals not only the love of God, but the power of God. And it also shows us the incomparable wisdom of God. To start to get at the wisdom of God at the cross, we have to rewind to the birth of Jesus and beyond. There is a little phrase in the New Testament that helps us get there: "fullness of time." We see it in Galatians 4:

But when the fullness of time had come, God sent forth his Son, born of woman, born under the law, to redeem those who were under the law, so that we might receive adoption as sons. (vv. 4–5 ESV)

The "fullness of time" is not so much a measure of seconds or days or years as it is a description of the times being right. Jesus was born at just the right time, at the very moment when God had completed bringing together every circumstance in the world to make it just so. Jesus knew this to be true, and he also operated under the "fullness of time" mentality.

Many times in Jesus' ministry, the crowds of people were more than willing to put him on their shoulders and march him into Jerusalem to declare him to be their King. They were under the mistaken idea that the Messiah was a political leader, come to overthrow their oppressors and reestablish the glory of Israel as it was under King David. To these crowds, clamoring for his coronation, Jesus denied their accolades and dispersed their enthusiasm under the banner of "my hour has not yet come" (John 2:4).

Jesus knew what he was about. And he was about death.

In both the Father and the Son, we see the immense wisdom it takes to deny a hurried opportunity in favor of God's will; to bring about circumstances to accomplish what they desire; to hold the course until the absolute perfect moment so the end game could be completed.

The cross demonstrates all these things and more. If worry and anxiety are a barometer of our faith, then the antidote is to have our faith bolstered. To do that, we must pry our eyes away from those circumstances that cast doubt on the wisdom, power, and love of God, and refocus them on the cross where those same attributes are proven once and for all.

Fish and Snakes and Fathers and Sons

Let's return, then, to the blessed state Jesus described in his sermon—that state in which the children of God, confident in the love, power, and wisdom of their Father, do not worry about what they will eat, or wear, or much of anything. This is how I want to live. I want to live unburdened by the things of the world, content with what comes from the Lord's hand, believing that regardless of what life looks like in the moment, it is ultimately for my good.

God, as our Father, only gives us fish and eggs—not scorpions and snakes. So says Jesus in Luke 11:

"What father among you, if his son asks for a fish, will give him a snake instead of a fish? Or if he asks for an egg, will give him a scorpion? If you then, who are evil, know how to give good gifts to your children, how much more will the heavenly Father give the Holy Spirit to those who ask him?" (vv. 11–13)

Because our eyes deceive us, we can't always recognize the difference between a fish and a snake. We might be fully convinced in our minds that what has come to us is a snake—it certainly stings like it is. In those moments, the children who are confident in their Father can step back and trust that it is truly a fish.

We can believe that God, as our Father, knows what is best for us. And because he does, we can accept what comes from his hand without anxiety. When we refocus our gaze on the cross, we can begin, over time, to grow down into the blessed state of peace that exists only for children.

CHAPTER 7

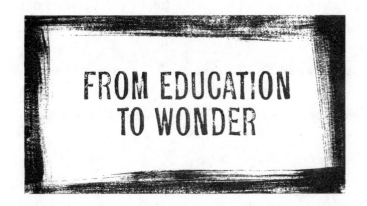

FROM EDUCATION TO WONDER

The Most Awesome . . . Until It's Not

One of the best parts about growing up in Texas, as I did, is history class. It might sound strange to you, but that's because you didn't grow up in the public school system of the Lone Star State. Any Texan can tell you that once every three years, state-adopted curriculum took you not to American history, and not to world history, but to Texas history.

Texas—the only state to fight its own war of independence.

Texas—the only state to actually be its own country.

Texas—the only state where Dr. Pepper was invented. You get the idea.

The crown jewel of Texas history is the Alamo. This was one of the most pivotal battles in the Texas Revolution, where some one hundred Texans refused to surrender their fort despite the fifteen hundred or so Mexican soldiers who laid siege to their garrison. The rebels defended the Alamo for thirteen days before it was finally taken. The battle cry, "Remember the Alamo!" was what the larger Texas army shouted during the Battle of San Jacinto when Texas won its independence.

I grew up hearing stories of Davy Crockett, who, despite being from Tennessee, found Texas so desirable that he relocated there and died defending the Alamo. I heard stories of Jim Bowie and his gigantic knife, who, even though he was near death, still fought off the Mexican soldiers to the very end. I heard stories of William Barrett Travis, who commanded the troops at the Alamo and famously wrote in a letter requesting reinforcements, "Victory or death."

Then came the summer when my family decided to go to San Antonio on our yearly vacation. While we were there, we would of course visit the Alamo, which still stands right in the heart of the city. I don't know what I expected to find there—something big. Something grand. Something worthy of all the stories of heroism I had heard for years.

What I got instead was a crumbling ten-foot wall with a little museum inside. The best thing the Alamo had to offer me, at that age, was an actual razor that had been used by Davy Crockett.

Yipee.

My disillusionment was only compounded as I later began to learn more and more about the people who fought inside that crumbling wall. Instead of being paragons of courage and virtue, defenders of liberty I had learned about, I heard stories of drunks, philanderers, debtors, and all other kinds of outlaws who were only in Texas because that was the only place left for them to go.

Funny how that happens, isn't it? As we grow older, we become more and more educated. But as we become more and more educated, a lot of the shine wears off of that which once captured our imaginations and filled us with wonder. For a kid, everything is awesome. As we grow into adulthood, we look everywhere for something that truly is.

Like so many other parts of growing up, this is natural. We are exposed to more and more as we age, and as we are exposed it takes more and more to actually impress us. And while that might be fine when it comes to historical sites, it's contrary to the kind of exuberant amazement that should fill the child of God regardless of how old they are. Just as our education in other matters slowly dilutes our wonder, our theological education can have the same effect—but for different reasons. While we might lose our wonder at things like historical sites because they don't measure up to what we had in our imaginations, we lose our wonder with the things of God due to familiarity. We pick and parse and dissect and discuss the wonder right out of ourselves.

The Over-Educated Christian

But education is a good thing, right? Aren't we to love God with our minds, as well as our hearts and our souls? True enough. I have been deeply affected by Christian thinkers like G. K. Chesterton, Charles Colson, C. S. Lewis, and others, who have argued in both explicit and implicit ways that Christians are to view their intellect as stewards view any other resource. From that viewpoint, the Christian should be the most educated they possibly can. To that end, I've pursued no small amount of religious education both formally and informally. It's precisely because of that commitment and education that I'm compelled to bring out this tendency I've seen in myself—namely, the loss of wonder.

This is applicable for many of us. There are no more educated people in the history of the world than we are, for there has been no greater access to education at any previous point in history.

My playlist abounds with countless sermons and unbridled access to biblical teaching. I live within a stone's throw of not one, not two, but at least three faithful, evangelical churches. The number of books by dead theologians on my bookshelves that I haven't even cracked far outnumber those I've read. At any given moment, I can be reading, listening to, or even watching centuries of commentary, study, and reflection on any biblical text I choose.

I am, if you'll excuse the metaphor, an intellectually fat Christian. My mind is obese with knowledge and bloated with facts. And I loosen the belt around my heavily churchified brain more and more day by day. Sadly, though, I've found that rarely does my passion keep pace with my knowledge; rarely does my heart walk in step with my mind. I don't think I'm alone. In fact, I can identify some distinct warning signs in myself to let me know that I'm drifting into the dangerous territory of knowing about God, and yet not being floored by the wonder of actually knowing God. These same warning signs might point to a similar loss of wonder and at the same time a high degree of education in your own life:

If you tend to have an attitude of examination rather than participation . . .

If you find yourself, surrounded by the worship of God, the preaching of the Word, and the fellowship of the saints, examining the methodology of those leading rather than participating in what's going on around you, it's very possible that you have begun to be overtaken by your education. In a case like that, you would prefer to analyze the details of the presentation rather than dwelling on and drinking deeply from the presence of God.

If you are more excited than grieved at finding fault . . .

If during that examination you do indeed find fault, and maybe it's something relatively minor, do you feel a sense of justification? I know that feeling, too. It's a sense of triumph that somehow you have been able to mine through all the external fluff and find that kernel of error that simply must be exposed. And if it's not exposed to the world, at least it's exposed in your own heart. When we feel that, we are feeding the animal of superiority that lurks in us all, that beast which craves a higher place over all others so that we might not feel so small, even for a moment.

If you desire generalities over personal specifics . . .

If, when you find yourself in a conversation with another in the body of Christ, there is no confession of sin, no admittance of struggle, and no grace to listen to another do the same, but instead a preference to deal in hypothetical "can God make a rock so big he couldn't move it" kind of discussions, then beware of over-education. In a case like this, we keep the truth of God and the conviction of the Holy Spirit at arm's length because we fear what might happen to us if it, and he, came any closer. Surely something would have to change, and we can't bear the thought of the magnifying glass of our gaze being turned inward.

It's the most terrible kind of irony to be surrounded by so much knowledge, and yet to no longer be awed by a single shred of it. It's something akin to floating in a raft in a freshwater sea, with the blazing sun beating down on you, and yet somehow not having the energy to stoop over the side of that raft to drink.

The Man Who Had It All

Solomon embodied this kind of despair. Here was a man who, more than anyone before or since, was surrounded by, well, everything. Every bit of learning. Every bit of pleasure. Every bit of sophistication. Every bit of everything. He was educated in all the ways of the world, and yet despite this extensive knowledge of everything under the sun, he found himself in a kind of malaise where nothing held wonder for him anymore. I resonate with that.

I know what it feels like to be in a constant funk. It's when you know intellectually that you should be more passionate and awestruck than you are, and yet you can't work it up inside yourself. The temptation,

I think, in those moments when the wonder is gone in the midst of excess, is to constantly pursue more. More books, more knowledge, more attendance, more wisdom—more of everything, as if adding excess on top of excess will bring about the simple wonder we once had as children. Or the simple amazement we once felt when we first believed that Jesus loves us because the Bible tells us so. But the answer to our lack of wonder is not found in addition of more and more. On the subject of education and study, Solomon himself said, "There is no end to the making of many books, and much study wearies the body" (Eccles. 12:12).

When I was in high school, my physics class was assigned a project that I'm sure was not unique to our school. We were given limited materials, mainly Popsicle sticks and wood glue, and were instructed to build a bridge with specific parameters. On the appointed day, all of us brought our bridges to class and they were placed over a gap between two desks. Then small weights were systematically hung to the bottom of the bridges to test and see how much weight they could bear. Of course, in that environment, the greatest thrill wasn't just winning the award for the sturdiest bridge, but also watching structure after structure be obliterated under the increasing weight.

The weights weren't added all at once; they were added slowly. One at a time. And they were added knowing that eventually every bridge would reach its capacity and crumble. No one thought that we could do something like stand on top of the bridge; though we didn't know how much, we knew they would be destroyed under far less weight than that of a person. These structures weren't made to support that kind of mass.

This is what the continual pursuit for more is like, and it's echoed in Ecclesiastes. In that book, Solomon systematically examined every part of life under the sun. He held up pleasure, work, time, knowledge, and even wisdom itself, and with each one, found it wanting. That's the recurrent refrain throughout the book after each aspect of life is examined—Meaningless! Vanity! Each and every time.

Each and every one of these pursuits were obliterated. Destroyed. Crushed under the weight. With each one, the Teacher found that they couldn't provide the kind of satisfaction we desire. And with each one, we find ourselves eventually and inevitably disappointed. Work never truly satisfies. Pleasure is never really enough. Knowledge is never really fulfilling. Like bridges in the high school physics class, they all eventually sagged and broke under the pressure.

So Solomon spent his life exhausting one pursuit after another, each time coming to the same conclusion—that we can't "educate" ourselves into joy, wonder, and fulfillment. The answer for our disen-chantment and apathy is not "more."

The life of Solomon stands in sharp contrast to another character of Scripture: John, who somehow, despite his age, wisdom, experience, and authority, never got over the simple but most profound truth of the existence of the Christian—that we are wholly and completely loved by God.

The Disciple Whom Jesus Loved

The love of God is the kind of mystery that one does not get over easily. It is the sort of mystery that grips and seizes the heart, one you can ponder day after day, and yet somehow know that you have never scratched the surface. It is the kind of mystery that so took hold of John, as a young disciple, and never let him go. It seems that John was drawn to this mysterious love of God in a special way, since he himself was known as the disciple who Jesus loved. And though he wrote about great theological issues, his thought process always took him back to this wondrous love of God.

The book John wrote near the end of his life, what we now call 1 John, was written to combat a heresy that had arisen that denied that Jesus was fully human. So John set out to show, based on his experience, that not only is Jesus God, but he is also fully man. But in the middle of his proof of the absolute physical reality of Jesus Christ, and subsequently how to be certain that one is his follower, he is again seized by the mystery that he has lived with his whole life, but can nevertheless escape.

This thought of a love so amazing, so divine, that we should be called children of God is so overpowering that John bursts forth in chapter three. My favorite rendition of the first verse of that chapter is found in the King James Version of the Bible: "Behold, what manner of love the Father hath bestowed upon us, that we should be called the sons of God." John says, "Look! Imagine! Consider! Believe! Wonder! Behold, what manner of love is this!"

John chose carefully his words in this sentence and used an expression that is unique in all of his writings: *potapan agapan*—What possible sort of love is this! The original meaning of this expression was, "of what country or race?" This is an expression used of things that are utterly foreign or unnatural. It is an expression that speaks of something unlike anything the human race has experienced. When confronted once again by the mystery, John's response is, "From what far realm did this love come? We sure haven't seen the likes of it around here!" And we certainly haven't.

Perhaps John was so continually amazed at this love of God because he knew what we know. Perhaps this love would be believable if it were given exclusively to kings and potentates. Maybe it would not be so alien and foreign if it were bestowed upon sweet little old ladies and innocent babies. But John knew what we know—he knew who we all were. He had seen our type before. Far from innocent children and sweet ladies, we were the selfish moneychangers and the Jews who demanded a sign back in chapter two of his Gospel. We were the Pharisee who was too afraid to approach Jesus in the daytime in chapter three. We were the Samaritan woman who has slept around her whole life in chapter four. We were the helpless, outcast paralytic in chapter five. We were the ones with stones in our hands to cast judgment out of hate and anger in chapter eight. We were the ones who got mad at those who show extraordinary emotion toward Jesus in chapter twelve. We were the ones who denied him in chapter eighteen. And we were the ones who cannot love him the way that he deserves to be loved in chapter twenty-one. John knew that we are unfaithful, unholy, unmerciful—he knew that we are undeserving.

But this love of God—this all-consuming, all-forgiving, all-accepting love of God—is not like anything else we have experienced. But that is the nature of this love. The Bible distinguishes between different types of love, and the main point of separation between these types are what prompts the love.

Most types of love are motivated by some external entity. That may be sexual desire, or self-interest, or self-preservation—but the point is that most types of love only occur when there is some benefit for the lover. But not this love. This love is sacrificial love. This love is freely given and expects nothing in return. This love is not given on the basis of the goodness of the one being loved, but on the goodness of the lover. How mysterious.

Knowing the Unknowable

Like Solomon, our education turns against us in the face of the mysterious love of God. For we are adults now, and we've long been educated in the ways of the world. And what our education has taught us is that this mystery of God's love, which maybe at one point captured our imaginations, is simply too good to be true. It does not make sense. Consequently, we either consciously or subconsciously tramp down the reality of the love of God in our minds until we become stale of heart. We might be able to recite the facts of the gospel, and yet we are no longer moved by them. We no longer survey the wondrous cross, though we have dissected it every which way from Sunday.

There exists, then, for the Christian, a balance to be had between the facts of the love of God, and the wonder at those facts. It is this mysterious balance between heart and head, between experience and intellect, that Paul prayed for the Ephesian church:

> For this reason I kneel before the Father from whom every family in heaven and on earth is named. I pray that he may grant you, according to the riches of his glory, to be strengthened with power in the inner man through his Spirit, and that Christ may dwell in your hearts through faith. I pray that you, being rooted and firmly established in love, may be able to comprehend with all the saints what is the length and width, height and depth of God's love, and to know Christ's love that surpasses knowledge, so you may be filled with all the fullness of God. (Eph. 3:14–19)

Paul prays that we would know that which is unknowable. Apparently we can, as God's children, know and yet not know at the same time. We can acknowledge but not fully grasp; we can study and yet not plumb the depths; we can believe and yet not fully understand. This is the beautiful, glorious way by which we are loved fully and wondrously as God's children.

But here is the trickiest part of all. How do we live in the middle of that mystery while still being awed by that mystery? In other words, how do we live in wonder and not presumption regarding the love of God? This is a very real danger, for we do it with countless other parts of our lives that we do not fully understand.

Take something as commonplace as a cell phone. I do not understand how a cell phone works. I don't even think about the fact that it does any more. But it is truly a wonder that I hold in my pocket a device through which I can speak to virtually anyone on the planet, access more information in a moment than previous generations could ever view in a lifetime, take pictures and make movies, and do countless other things.

All this I simply accept without wonder anymore. In fact, the only time I do think about it is when I'm inconvenienced because it doesn't work quickly enough. This is the danger we can drift into when we lose our wonder. Though we might know all the ins and outs of God's love, we begin to presume upon its reality. And the result is a very educated, but very cold heart. It is the same kind of heart that characterized the church in Ephesus in the book of Revelation.

Return to Your First Love

If we fast-forward a few decades, we see a very different picture of the church at Ephesus than the one

Paul knew. It was for this church that Paul prayed a grand experience in the love of God—indeed, that they would know the love that surpasses knowledge. And yet some years later, it seems this wonder that characterized the church had all but been snuffed out. This is what the Lord Jesus said about the church:

> "I know your works, your labor, and your endurance, and that you cannot tolerate evil people. You have tested those who call themselves apostles and are not, and you have found them to be liars. I know that you have persevered and endured hardships for the sake of my name, and have not grown weary. But I have this against you: You have abandoned the love you had at first. Remember then how far you have fallen; repent, and do the works you did at first. Otherwise, I will come to you and remove your lampstand from its place, unless you repent." (Rev. 2:2–5)

Jesus had no issue with the conduct of these Christians. They were working, laboring, and enduring. They refused to tolerate evil and were very accurate theologically, even going so far as testing and putting out those found to be doctrinally deficient. And yet they were cold. And despite all their accolades, Jesus said that they were in great danger.

This is a fearsome thing to all of us grown-ups in the faith—that we might say the right thing, know the right thing, even defend the right thing, and yet have the Lord Jesus hold our lack of love against us. But if you, in all your education, sense the same rebuke coming to you in this moment, there is hope, just as there was hope for this church. And Jesus tells us just how to grow up in our love and wonder.

The first thing involves remembering. In this case, Jesus says the church should remember how far they have fallen. Remembering is a powerful discipline for us to get back what has been lost. When passion wanes in your marriage, spend some time remembering. When friendships are on the rocks, spend some time remembering. When you're questioning the faithfulness of God, spend some time remembering. Call to mind intentionally and repetitively moments from your past, and use those moments to fuel your present.

Surely we can do this as we look back over our lives. We can remember the days when we were dead in our sin. We can call to mind the moments when God awakened us to his great love in Christ. We can recall with clarity moments in worship when we have been overcome with gratitude and awe. But we can't stop at remembering; we must also repent, just as the church at Ephesus had to do.

What does it mean to repent? Contrary to popular belief, "repent" does not mean "stop." It means "turn." It means we were walking in one direction and we turn and walk in another. In this case, it means that though we might have been walking in an educated, informed, and even correct fashion, we were not walking into the wondrous loving arms of Jesus. So we must turn, and when we do, we find ourselves in a situation just like the prodigal son who has rehearsed all the things he is going to do to make his father love him when he is tackled before he gets to the front porch. We find a Father who falls upon our neck and welcomes us back.

We remember. Then we repent. And finally, we act. We "do the works you did at first" (Rev. 2:5). What did we do at first, when we were newly born-again children, overcome with wonder at God's love? We sang freely. We worshipped regularly. We immersed ourselves in God's Word to know him. We extended the same love to others that we had received from God. These are the things we do once again in our repentance.

These things—these simple expressions that one time flowed so naturally out of an overflowing heart—these are the kindling the Lord uses to build the fire of our love and wonder again.

These are the things that return us to the cross, where Jesus bought our renewed love relationship and unconditional acceptance with God when he exclaimed,

"My God, my God, why have you forsaken me?" The punishment that was upon him bought us peace. The suffering that he endured bought our inheritance. And because of that cry, we as the church together with John live our lives in the shadow of the mystery of the love of God.

And we, too, now cry out not once but continually. And our cry is not one of pain, but of joy. It is not out of broken relationship but out of unmerited favor. And as we sit someday in our justified, sanctified, and glorified bodies around the table, we will still cry with wonder. And the words will mirror those words that he uttered so long ago on the cross—but we will say, "My God, my God, why have you accepted me?" As we sit at that table, the mystery will finally be solved. When faith becomes sight and we finally sit at the table where we truly belong, the mystery will be solved. We will wonder no more, for the answer to that question can only be found in the Lamb slain before the foundation of the world who then will sit at the head of that table. He himself is the answer to our question.

We are, thanks to Him, the children of God. Those who didn't "get over it." Those who again and again were filled with an exuberant amazement at this God who loves us so deeply.

CHAPTER 8

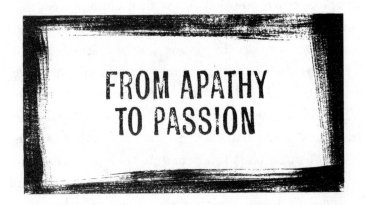

The Day the Tears Stop Flowing

I don't remember the last time I cried at school, but I do remember making the conscious choice not to. When I was in seventh grade, I broke my wrist on the football practice field. The fracture hurt worse than any pain I had experienced up to that point, and to make matters worse, it happened at the very beginning of practice. Though in the moment I wanted nothing more than to burst into tears and beg the coaches to call my parents, I instead chose to heed the teenage warning that reverberated in my mind. I can still remember the mantra to this day: *Don't cry. Only babies cry.*

I didn't cry that day. Instead, I stood on the sidelines of practice for two more hours until my parents came to pick me up. As a dad, I have seen this same tendency to choke down emotion in my own children. As they continue to get older, I've noticed that the occasions when they cry are becoming less and less frequent. Replacing the tears is that screwed-up facial expression as they try and hold back the waterworks. Whether the source of the tears is a physical or an emotional pain, they have started to lock it away, and only the most rogue of single tears can penetrate their defenses.

This is what happens when we move from the age of childhood into the pre-teen zone, and our lack of tears is but one example. We become "too cool" for virtually any display of emotion. The greatest of joys only elicits a smirk, and the worst sadness or embarrassment only brings the slightest shade of red on our faces. We bury our emotions deeply as we get older, increasingly afraid of allowing any crack in our carefully constructed image to show.

That's not all bad. As adults, we need to be more even-keeled. We simply can't function together in maturity when everything is either the best or the worst thing of all time, when our logic is blinded by our mood, and our ability to navigate life is shaded by emotional swings. And yet there is something we are missing as adults. We miss the passion of childhood in which we are truly joyful, truly excited, truly passionate about all kinds of things. But in his great work, the Lord redeems the emotions of his children, and in his kingdom we find ourselves growing down in our apathy and growing up in this passion we've lost as we've gotten older.

Asparagus and the Crushing Command of Affection

Jesus commands affection from his followers. In fact, this command of affection is really the summation of all his other commands. Jesus, in Matthew 22, sums up the entire Law in just two simple statements:

> "Love the Lord your God with all your heart, with all your soul, and with all your mind. This is the greatest and most important command. The second is like it: Love your neighbor as yourself. All the Law and the Prophets depend on these two commands." (vv. 37–40)

At first glance, this might actually seem encouraging. If we are tempted to look at the Bible as an endless series of commands from God (which, by the way, it is not), we might take comfort in the fact that Jesus nutshells the whole thing for us here. He unraveled the centuries of qualifications and amendments that the religious leaders of his day had wrapped around their religion and boiled it down very succinctly: Love God. Love your neighbor. That's it. But when you begin to consider the matter more deeply, you realize just how crushing this command from Jesus really is.

By way of illustration, consider a scenario that almost every parent has faced—asparagus night. My own children are no great fans of asparagus—not the color, not the texture, and certainly not the taste. Unfortunately for them, their parents really like it, and so it's not uncommon for a plate of freshly grilled asparagus to be served at dinner. That's when the battle of wills begins.

On asparagus night, it's a test of persevering stubbornness to see who will break first—the parents, or the kids. Everything else on the plate will be eaten, until there will be left only the lonely green stalks on three plates, and there it will sit. And sit. And sit. Until it starts to get cold and mushy, and the act of eating the asparagus will move from being distasteful to downright disgusting. The only question at that point is who can play the waiting game longer. At some point, inevitably, I will have to put my hands on the table, look my children in the eyes, and say clearly: "You will eat that asparagus."

In the end, though, our kids are (mainly) compliant. They will eat the asparagus. Sure, it will be with plenty of drama as they force feed it to themselves one bite at a time, washed down with gallons of whatever drink they have, but after a couple of hours they will eventually get it down. They will obey my command and go through the mechanics of eating what I tell them to eat.

But let's say that one night—one asparagus night—I decided to change the game. So the table is set. The food is dispersed. And there again sits the asparagus on each of their plates. That's when it gets interesting, because this time, I do not say, "Eat the asparagus." Instead, I say, "Tonight, kids, I give you a new command. *Love your asparagus.*"

This is indeed a game-changer. And if the kids were self-aware enough to do so, the most honest way they could respond to me would be something like this:

"Daddy, you have given us an impossible command. If you told us to eat the asparagus, we can force ourselves into obedience. But you're asking us for something much different than that—something we cannot do. So if you are going to give us this command, then you must also be able to give us new taste buds to go along with it." Which leads us back to the crushing command of affection from Jesus in Matthew 22.

Can These Dry Bones Live?

Though Jesus' summation of the law might seem simple, all those who hear it must honestly look to the

Son of God with the same eyes of desperation I can see in my mind's eye from my own children. Like them, we have to respond, "Jesus, you have given us a crushing command. We can go through the mechanics of so many religious actions, but not this. We cannot will ourselves to victory here. If you are giving us this crushing command, we need a new heart to go along with it."

To which Jesus smiles, and says, "Yes."

There is a powerful scene recorded for us in the book of Ezekiel that illustrates the life-giving power of the gospel, which answers this command of Jesus. In Ezekiel 37, God's prophet was brought by the Spirit of God to a valley of death in order to be shown something miraculous:

> The hand of the LORD was on me, and he brought me out by his Spirit and set me down in the middle of the valley; it was full of bones. He led me all around them. There were a great many of them on the surface of the valley, and they were very dry. Then he said to me, "Son of man, can these bones live?"
>
> I replied, "Lord GOD, only you know." (vv. 1–3)

The Lord asks a penetrating question, doesn't he? Can these dry bones live? Can that which is lifeless come to life again? Can the dusty remnants have flesh once more? Can the dryness of age be rejuvenated with youth? And the prophet answered rightly: "Lord God, only you know."

The scene continues, and Ezekiel bears witness to the sound of the bones starting to rattle. Then he hears the "click, click, click" as these dry bones start to latch together. Then tendons and flesh started to grow and wrap around the skeletons until before him was a vast fleshly army—covered in skin, but still dead. But then the breath of life entered into these cadavers and they stood, alive, before Ezekiel.

What was lifeless became a mighty army. What was dry and dusty was warm and tender. What was brittle and hard became pliable and soft. Here is the Lord's conclusion of the vision:

> "Son of man, these bones are the whole house of Israel. Look how they say, 'Our bones are dried up, and our hope has perished; we are cut off.' Therefore, prophesy and say to them: 'This is what the Lord GOD says: I am going to open your graves and bring you up from them, my people, and lead you into the land of Israel. You will know that I am the LORD, my people, when I open your graves and bring you up from them. I will put my Spirit in you, and you will live, and I will settle you in your own land. Then you will know that I am the LORD. I have spoken, and I

will do it. This is the declaration of the LORD.'"
(Ezek. 37:11–14)

This vision was immediately applicable to God's people who, because of their disobedience, were in a lifeless state. They were exiled from their homeland, their temple destroyed, wondering if God had abandoned them. There was no love, no passion, no hope—only the dry bones of what once was. But God brings life from the most hopeless of situations.

This same scene is played out every time someone believes the gospel. In desperation, we recognize that we do not have the capacity to do what Jesus requires of us. Our hearts are ruined, bent toward sin, and lifeless as a valley of dry bones. But by his grace, God brings life to our dusty souls. When we are born again in Christ, our emotions are born again as well, and this new heart that God gives us can actually begin to beat in rhythm with his Spirit. Because of the gospel, we can actually love God.

One chapter earlier, just before God gave his prophet the vision of dry bones, he told him clearly that this heart-level change would happen: "I will give you a new heart and put a new spirit within you; I will remove your heart of stone and give you a heart of flesh. I will place my Spirit within you and cause you to follow my statutes and carefully observe my ordinances" (Ezek. 36:26–27).

Thanks to the gospel, our capacity for love has been brought from death to life. But the redemption that the Lord brings to his children does not stop with spiritual life. If we look back to the words of Jesus in Matthew 22, we see that it is a whole and complete kind of love. We are to love him with everything we are—with our emotions, our intellect, even our physical bodies. Everything we do, think, and feel is an expression of this new right relationship with God. This means that God is day-by-day bringing redemption to our entire emotional lives. He is bringing us back from the apathy that resounds so deeply in the cold, dead heart, that emotional guardedness that keeps us from feeling anything deeply and fully. He is replacing it with a tenderness that is unique to the Christian experience. He is bringing us back to what it means to be a child—not one who has been corrupted by sin, but one who has been made new in the kingdom. Because of this, the Christian should feel emotion more deeply than anyone else.

Joy

I can think of several examples of the kind of emotional engagement that is deeper for the Christian than for anyone else. Leading that list for the Christian is joy. The child of God should feel a deeper sense of joy than anyone else because the Christian is uniquely positioned to know the true source of joy more than anyone else.

Joy is one of those things we tend to confuse with something else. Happiness, satisfaction, pleasure—these are all fine things, but they are not joy. Not really. Joy is distinct from any other emotional experience because joy does not wax and wane with circumstances. This is because joy runs deeper than a mere sentiment; while a sentiment or a sensation might ebb and flow depending on what's happening at a given moment, joy finds its true source in God and in God alone. As we grow in Christ, then, our joy increases—not because our lives get better and better circumstantially, but because our knowledge of and relationship with God deepens as we grow. As the psalmist said,

> You reveal the path of life to me; in your presence is abundant joy; at your right hand are eternal pleasures. (Ps. 16:11)

Because the source of joy is not circumstance but instead God himself, we can know that our true source of joy will never be shaken. No matter what else happens, no matter how much or little money, health, or anything else we have, we will always and forever be rich in Christ. That means we are never ultimately without hope. Don't confuse joy with optimism or some pie-in-the-sky version of tomorrow. Joy comes with the morning because God is still there, even if nothing else is. Again, from the psalmist:

> For his anger lasts only a moment, but his favor, a lifetime. Weeping may stay overnight, but there is joy in the morning. (Ps. 30:5)

But for the same reason joy is stable, we must remember that joy is not found through immediate gratification, but by pushing past it. This is contrary to happiness, which is found around every corner. We see peddlers of emotion on billboards, commercials, and a host of other places. Everywhere we turn, the promise of happiness is held out for us. But joy is deeper. C. S. Lewis once made the comparison between happiness and joy by saying that we are content to play around making mudpies because we have no concept of a holiday at the sea. In other words, our issue is that we are far too easily pleased. We can find true joy when we become discontent and dissatisfied with temporary sources of happiness and find ourselves pushing past immediate gratification into the source of true joy.

It may be latent inside you, Christian, but the capacity for true joy is there because the Holy Spirit is there. This capacity for joy is only for the Christian to feel, and feel deeply, for the Christian alone has the glorious access to the source of that joy.

Justice

Not only should the Christian feel joy more deeply than anyone else, but the Christian should feel a sense of justice more acutely than anyone else. We see echoes of this sense of justice in ourselves as children, or at least within our own kids. There was a day, as children, when we could not imagine a story in which good didn't win and the bad guy didn't get what he deserved. In our own house there are still audible cheers that go up at the end of every Disney movie when the bad guy finally gets what's coming to him or her.

But as adults, we know that the good guy doesn't always win. We've seen it happen so many times that we aren't even surprised any more. Our feelings resemble that of the psalmist in Psalm 73:

> God is indeed good to Israel, to the pure in heart. But as for me, my feet almost slipped; my steps nearly went astray. For I envied the arrogant; I saw the prosperity of the wicked. They have an easy time until they die, and their bodies are well fed. They are not in trouble like others; they are not afflicted like most people. Therefore, pride is their necklace, and violence covers them like a garment. Their eyes bulge out from fatness; the imaginations of their hearts run wild. They mock, and they speak

maliciously; they arrogantly threaten oppression. They set their mouths against heaven, and their tongues strut across the earth. Therefore his people turn to them and drink in their overflowing words. The wicked say, "How can God know? Does the Most High know everything?" Look at them—the wicked! They are always at ease, and they increase their wealth. (vv. 1–12)

The psalmist looked around the world and felt an acute sense of injustice. The wicked were prospering all around him, and everything in him rose up in a collective, "It's not fair!" As the psalm continues, we see that his attitude was changed, but notice that it wasn't that he suddenly stopped desiring justice for the wicked. Instead, the change came through a vision of eternity:

Did I purify my heart and wash my hands in innocence for nothing? For I am afflicted all day long and punished every morning. If I had decided to say these things aloud, I would have betrayed your people. When I tried to understand all this, it seemed hopeless until I entered God's sanctuary. Then I understood their destiny. Indeed, you put them in slippery places; you make them fall into ruin. How suddenly they become a desolation! They come to an end, swept away by terrors. Like one waking from a dream, Lord, when arising, you will despise their image. (vv. 13–20)

The presence of God did not diminish the desire for justice in the psalmist; the presence of God made him more confident that justice would ultimately be served. As Christians, we are confident in the God of eternity, and as such, we can trust that he will ultimately and completely set things as they should be. This truth actually compels us to feel the need for justice more deeply because our desire for justice is not grounded in something as trivial as jealousy or revenge. In a redeemed state, we want justice because we have come to love and treasure the holiness of God. This is what is eternally offended by the perpetrations of injustice in this current life.

The reason why the Christian can do things like turn the other cheek, meet insult with love, and rejoice in the midst of persecution, is because we are confident that eternity is real. We know that one day, finally, God will do what is right by all.

Grief

The Christian should not only feel joy and justice more passionately than anyone else; the Christian should grieve more deeply and meaningfully than anyone else. Paul's commentary on grief is found in 1 Thessalonians 4:13: "We do not want you to be uninformed, brothers and sisters, concerning those who are asleep, so that you will not grieve like the rest, who have no hope."

Notice that the apostle never says we should not grieve; he says the manner in which we grieve should be very different than those who do not believe in Jesus. Grief is good and right and necessary. In fact, Christians should be the best at grieving. The first reason why is stated in the verse—because we grieve more hopefully than anyone else.

Grief is about loss. And while we primarily think of grief in terms of losing a person, we can also grieve other things—a dream, a career, a relationship—pretty much anything we have a deep association with. Whenever that thing is taken from us, we feel a void in its place—and that's exactly how we should feel. But as Christians, our grief is always tempered with a sense of expectation, because we hope in a day when grief will be a thing of the past, because loss will be a thing of the past. When Christians grieve, then, they don't grieve despairingly; they grieve hopefully, because Jesus—through his life, death, and resurrection—has shown us that death is not the final word.

The Christian grieves with one eye on the coffin and one eye on the empty tomb.

But there's another reason why Christians grieve differently; this one, though, is not quite as expected as the first. I believe Christians can (and should) grieve more deeply than others. The reason we grieve more deeply is because Christians understand and embrace that suffering and the loss it creates is not random; it's not by happenstance; and it's not some kind of cosmic accident. Christians know that ultimately all suffering comes from sin. When sin entered the world, every-thing in the created order was broken. As a result, there is grief. So when we grieve, we are doing something more profound than crying for a singular loss; we are mourning the entire state of creation. We are recogniz-ing that with this death, with this disappointment, with this disease, we are beholding yet another example of how things were not supposed to be.

We mourn and groan not only for our own loss, but for the entire state of creation. In our grief, the hope of the resurrection holds hands with the sorrow of the crucifixion, so we grieve and rejoice in ways that point to the terrible nature of sin and the greatness of the redemption that's on its way.

Don't Trust Your Feelings

The child of God should feel more, not less, than the person of the world. As the redeemed sons and daughters of God, our emotions are born anew into Christ, and the sanctifying work of the Holy Spirit applies not only to our actions, but also to those emotions. As we are day by day transformed into the image of Jesus, we also day by day begin to feel the right things. But the progress is slow.

Tomorrow morning, rest assured that neither you nor I will wake up and *feel* exactly the way we are supposed to feel. We will get angry at the wrong things, feel pleasure in the wrong things, and not be saddened enough by the right things. This is because the work of the Spirit is ongoing, but not complete. In the meantime, we would do well to recognize that we cannot— we must not—trust our feelings.

Even when we recognize this fact, there is still the temptation for us to take the stance of victim when it comes to the way we feel. We feel happy or sad or faithful or unfaithful in a given moment. When we feel, we often just go with the feeling, or else we play the victim to those feelings, believing there is nothing we can do about it. But in order to grow up in the right kind of emotion and grow down in apathy, we must take an active stance against our feelings when we know those feelings run contrary to the revealed will of God. We must choose to go to battle against our own hearts, and in so doing surrender ourselves to the redemptive work of the Holy Spirit. So how do we do that? I'd suggest three ways.

First of all, we can choose to anticipate the right things. While you might not be able to directly control what you feel, you can control what you choose to look forward to. And all of us are anticipating something. It might be as simple as an evening at home or a planned vacation, but all of us have some fixed point in the future we are anticipating. When we look forward to something, we begin to desire to see that thing take place.

In light of that, one way we battle against our feelings is to consciously choose to anticipate the things of God. We can make the choice to put our focus on the coming of Jesus' kingdom, the righting of all wrongs in that kingdom, or even something as simple as meeting weekly with the people of God. When we make the choice to anticipate the right things over and over again, we will begin to see ourselves actually develop a deep level of affection for that which we are anticipating.

Second, we can practice the discipline of gratitude. Gratitude is more than a feeling; it's a discipline. That's why we are not told in Scripture to feel thankful, but instead commanded to give thanks in all circumstances, for this is God's will for us in Christ (1 Thess. 5:18). Even when we don't feel thankful, and even when we feel that we have to search for something to be thankful for, we can still engage in this discipline.

Personally, I have at different seasons implemented this discipline through a daily journal entry in which I record at least three things I'm thankful for. More than once, I have fallen back on something like, "I'm thankful that the Lord has not left me today," or "I'm thankful that the gospel is still true today." But these are not just easy answers; they instead are actual spiritual realities I can choose to thank the Lord for even if I don't feel it. In my own experience, by practicing this discipline, my feelings have eventually followed, and not only am I practicing gratitude but actually feeling thankful.

We can battle our wrong feelings through anticipating the right things. And we can battle our feelings through practicing gratitude. One final way we can battle our feelings is through the simple, but defiant act of singing. Singing like children. It's very encouraging to me to see that I'm not the only one who feels double-minded when it comes to their feelings; that others, like me, have a certain way they want to feel, and yet do not. More encouraging still is that the psalmist struggled with the same thing. Psalms 42 and 43 especially record such feelings for us, but they also record a songwriter not content to simply feel what he feels, but rather to take an active role in it. In these passages, then, you find the psalmist not just talking to his own soul, but actually singing to it:

Why, my soul, are you so dejected? Why are
you in such turmoil? Put your hope in God, for
I will still praise him, my Savior and my God.
(Ps. 42:5)

There is something that connects our hearts with
our heads through music. We may know what we ought
to feel in our minds, know the truth of God's character
and his Word, and yet not feel it deeply; but music is a
tool to help it. Music can lift the heart and connect the
head. So one simple way, then, we can take an active
role in what we feel, is to sing the truth. Over and over
again.

There will come a day, friends, when like children,
we will be rightly passionate about the exact right
things. Until that day, we can grow down in the apathy
that is so systemic among adults. We can choose to
stoke the fire of good and godly emotion, trusting that
the Holy Spirit will bring along our redeemed hearts
to glory.

CHAPTER 9

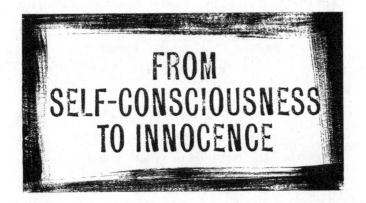

Deodorant, Hairbrushes, and Mouthwash

When did you start brushing your teeth? I mean really brushing them. Not the perfunctory molar skimming, but a real, intentional, deep cleaning of those teeth. Do you remember? Now think back before then. Think back before the dreaded days of puberty, when kids not only can get by with no deodorant, undone hair, and minimally brushed teeth—think back to the days when the lack of these things is actually cute on a kid.

These were the days of mismatched socks, pants that are too short, crazy, unkempt hair—it's just part of the overall package that makes kids so endearing to us. After all, who has time to worry about issues of personal hygiene when Daniel Tiger is teaching important life lessons? See? Cute.

But then, for all of us, these things started to matter . . . a lot. Sadly, that moment came just a few months too late for most. Thanks to one comment from that one girl or guy, our whole sense of self comes into question. Almost overnight, we move from a state of blissful freedom into a state of heightened drama. Things like our appearance become matters of national security as we ponder the mystery of what so-and-so is wearing and whether we should follow suit. Thus begins our lifelong struggle with personal insecurity, for thus began our first blush with self-awareness.

As we continue to grow up, we become less and less secure about more and more stuff. We become masters of second-guessing, whereby we evaluate every comment, every outfit choice, every conversation, every interaction, time and time again. We replay in our minds what we've said, worn, tweeted, posted, or displayed, each time wondering if we said, wore, or posted it just right. As adults, we are held in bondage by a preoccupation regarding our own image, living as slaves to the fear of what others might or might not think of us.

It is not so with children. It's not that children consciously reject what others think about them; it's something more beautiful than that. Children live in a state of self-forgetfulness, where they are what they are and say what they say. They are, in this sense, very free, for they are not bound by the self-consciousness that dominates so many of our moment-by-moment decisions as adults. We are in chains to our own image, and our bondage is manifested in personal insecurity. The truly ironic part about this bondage is that we have convinced ourselves of the great virtue of self-awareness to the point that we are spending thousands of dollars and thousands more hours of time chasing after a greater and greater degree of self-awareness. Though self-consciousness brings all kinds of insecurity, second-guessing, and general paranoia, most adults continue deeper down the rabbit hole of introspection.

Self-Awareness Is Not an End in Itself

To be clear, self-awareness is not a bad thing in and of itself. In fact, knowing yourself is actually inter-twined with knowing God. John Calvin wrote in the beginning of *Institutes of the Christian Religion* these words in regard to knowledge of God and knowledge of self:

> Our wisdom, in so far as it ought to be deemed true and solid wisdom, consists almost entirely of two parts: the knowledge of God and of our-selves. But as these are connected together by

many ties, it is not easy to determine which of the two precedes and gives birth to the other.[7]

I've found this experience to be true; self-awareness and God-awareness are linked together. That's not to say, however, they are the same thing. God and humanity are different from each other, and the pathway to God is NOT found through exploring oneself. At the same time, the link is strong. As one begins to plumb the depths of who God is, one inevitably has the same experience as Isaiah in Isaiah 6. In the light of the knowledge of God we are forced to recognize the true depth of our own depravity. And as we see ourselves in light of him, we are again forced to reflect on who he is, as he is different from who we are.

And so the circle goes. As we know more and more of God, we also become more and more aware of ourselves. And as we become more and more aware of ourselves, we look increasingly at the character of God.

Self-awareness is a good thing, then, for all kinds of reasons. For one thing, it forces us to recognize in our faults that God exists apart from those faults. For example, we might find in ourselves a desire for justice to be done in the world, and yet through our increasing self-awareness we recognize that we want this justice to be done to others at the exclusion of ourselves. It's good for everyone else to be held accountable, just not ourselves. But God is not like that.

Another reason self-awareness is a good thing is because of the effect on our relationships with others. We can be more sympathetic and compassionate toward others when we recognize the same characteristic at play in our own lives. But this self-awareness is not an end in itself. That's because that rabbit hole of self-discovery, if we are truly honest with ourselves, doesn't lead to self-actualization. It leads to despair.

Know Thyself . . . If You Dare

Both Socrates and Plato are credited with the phrase, "Know thyself." These same two words have also become a mantra taken up in the modern day. In so many words, all kinds of gurus from all kinds of perspectives are saying the same thing—know thyself, and then obey thyself. That is, the chief end of mankind is to understand what makes you uniquely happy, and then to pursue that happiness regardless of what stands in your way.

Of course, there is an assumption behind this philosophy. It is assumed that when we end up knowing ourselves, we will find a great deal of freedom and release and gratification. But what happens when self-awareness leads you where you don't want to go? What if you subscribe to the philosophy, and yet at the end of it, you are broken by what you find? This is the true end of self-awareness, at least when we are honest with ourselves. Because it is, it's no wonder that all the adults who have gotten into this endless rabbit hole of self-exploration find they are never satisfied, never truly actualized, and always teetering on the brink of despair. In the Bible, this is what happened to Peter, one who came face-to-face with what he was truly capable of—and it left him devastated.

Peter was so sure of himself. He was the one who confessed Jesus as the Messiah. He was the one who had walked on water. He was the one who had come to Christ's defense with the sword in the garden—and that last one happened after Jesus cast doubt on his commitment. He heard the words about his denials in the back of his mind as he slashed at the soldier. Three times, indeed.

But then it happened. In a matter of a few hours, Peter saw the truth about himself. He came face-to-face with the fact that he was not nearly as strong, not nearly as faithful, not nearly as committed, as he would have liked to believe. And the truth of himself made him weep bitterly.

I remember many years ago, I was pushing a lawnmower. And for the first time, and seemingly out of nowhere, I had my own "rooster" moment. I saw with vivid clarity the fact that all my religious actions, all my friendships, all the good things I had done, were really about me. They were all done, at least at some level, to make people like me. Or think well of me. Or be impressed with me. And the lawnmower got very difficult to push much further.

It is a frightening thing to look inside oneself. There's nothing quite as devastating as realizing with sudden clarity just what you are capable of. It's in those moments that the "good news" of self-exploration and the idea that true joy and happiness can be found with knowing, and then obeying, oneself is proven false. The lie is exposed when we peel back the layers of our personhood. And we are left, like Peter, like me, with a sense of bankruptcy. We cry as the prophet did, "Woe is me! For we are unclean people, and we come from an unclean people" (see Isa. 6:5). Self-awareness—true self-awareness—will lead us to a place we don't want to go.

Now there are two options when we come to the realization of what we are capable of. On the one hand, we can simply carry on as we have been, walking further and further down the road of self-discovery. But if left unchecked, our self-awareness will quickly become self-idolatry.

We will become our own God; we are the object of our pursuits. This, unfortunately, is the unintended result of our emphasis on "authenticity" and "community." We become people who justify our sin and our

shortcomings because they are known and acknowledged and shared with others. We no longer feel conviction about this stuff in our lives that has yet to be
fully claimed by the gospel because our struggles are
common and even understandable.

Alternatively, we can come to the uncomfortable
realization of just who we are and what we are capable
of, and then find ourselves in just the right position to
find true freedom through Jesus. The freedom Jesus
brings is not only freedom from sin and death—it's also
freedom from this kind of self-worship masquerading
as introspection.

True Freedom

We are free in Christ. This is our calling as the children of God. That freedom comes with opportunity,
though, and not all the opportunity is for good: "For
you were called to be free, brothers and sisters; only
don't use this freedom as an opportunity for the flesh,
but serve one another through love" (Gal. 5:13).

According to Paul, we might look at this freedom
we have through Christ, this freedom from sin, death,
judgment, condemnation, and a host of other perilous
shackles, and not respond in a way befitting that freedom. We might see our freedom as an opportunity for
the flesh.

This might mean that we become not just recipients of grace, but abusers of grace. We might look to the cross, whereby God has given us this great pardon, and see the forgiveness of Jesus as an endless license to do whatever pleases us at a moment. We might reason, *If God has forgiven me for everything—past, present, and future—then my actions really have no consequences. I'm free to pursue all my pleasure, and then throw up an occasional "Forgive me," and I'm good to go.* The Bible has a word for that kind of attitude:

> For some people, who were designated for this judgment long ago, have come in by stealth; they are ungodly, turning the grace of our God into sensuality and denying Jesus Christ, our only Master and Lord. (Jude 4)

But there are other ways we might see the freedom we have in Christ as an opportunity for the flesh. "The flesh" is more than just gratifying our desires for things like sex, money, and power—"the flesh" is that part of us that cries out for our own self-lordship and self-determination. It's that part of us that still considers us to be the center of the universe. And if we are at the center of the universe, then everyone and everything else must bend to our will. The mind-set that characterizes this kind of person is one that is wholly and completely centered on self. And while that self-centeredness might take the form of self-gratification, it might also take more sinister forms. Forms like self-consciousness.

It's a little counterintuitive to think in this way, but our heightened self-consciousness is really just a sanitized mask for our own preoccupation with self. Think of it like this:

Let's say that you wake up tomorrow morning, and you know you have an important meeting. This is the kind of meeting that you will remember for years to come. Maybe it's a job interview. Or perhaps it's a great networking opportunity. Maybe it's that moment when you tell another person something significant about your relationship. Because of the importance of this meeting, you get dressed. Then you look in the mirror. Then you get dressed again. And again. And again. And when you finally do leave the house, you are still not comfortable with what you're wearing. In fact, you spend the entire rest of the day second-guessing your clothing choices, worrying about what this particular ensemble will communicate about you.

Now you might spin a situation like this to the angle of responsibility. You want to make a good impression, and so you spent considerable time thinking about what you wear with that intention. Or you might spin it to the angle of humility. You have a low opinion of yourself, and are certainly not proud of the way you look. But either way you spin it, you cannot spin it as though it were for the benefit of the other person you were meeting with. Your focus was never on that person, though you might talk yourself into believing it was. It was on you. Your outfit. Your image. And the only consideration you gave to another was the opinion they might form of you as a result of your clothing choice.

This is not the kind of freedom Christ has brought to us. Instead, Jesus frees us by giving us a new master. And this new Master is great enough to drive out our obsession with ourselves and free us to truly love and serve him and others. That new Master, then, reframes what self-awareness looks like. Ironically, the maturing of self-awareness takes us back to childhood, for the maturing of self-awareness is not self-knowledge—it's self-forgetfulness.

Know Thyself . . . and Forget Thyself

Like all other parts of our lives, there is a certain kind of maturity to our self-awareness that happens as we grow in Christ. The maturing of our self-awareness is, ironically, self-forgetfulness. This, in the end, is what true humility is made of.

Here, too, we have some confusion, because we tend to think that humility means thinking we are worthless. It means the deflection of compliments and a refusal to accept that we might be good at doing a particular thing. Instead of simply saying "thank you" when someone offers us a word of encouragement, we brush it off, all the while longing in our souls that someone else will pick up the compliment and continue the conversation on our behalf. Or that by our deflection, we will actually intensify the admiration of another, so that they think we are not only good at a particular thing, but also really good at being humble.

Messed up, right? Right.

Part of self-awareness is knowing that we are, in fact, good at things. But the other side of that coin is being aware that even when we are doing something that seems to be pretty selfless in the moment, our motives are tainted with vain conceit and self-indulgence. We serve, but we want to be acknowledged for our service. We pray and study, but we want others to recognize how much we've done. We give, but we feel slighted when we aren't recognized for what we've done.

This is where the maturing of our self-awareness comes in. By God's grace, hopefully we are moving in the direction where we know ourselves more and yet think of ourselves less. So how does that happen? The answer is really one of focus:

> Therefore, since we also have such a large cloud of witnesses surrounding us, let us lay

aside every hindrance and the sin that so easily ensnares us. Let us run with endurance the race that lies before us, keeping our eyes on Jesus, the source and perfecter of our faith. For the joy that lay before him, he endured the cross, despising the shame, and has sat down at the right hand of the throne of God. (Heb. 12:1–2)

How do you move from self-consciousness to innocence? From self-lordship to self-forgetfulness? Fix your eyes on Jesus. Of course, when we hear that, the cynic inside all of us rises up and says, "Yeah, but . . ." It sounds too simple, doesn't it? Got to be more to it? But perhaps the simplicity in and of itself is what gives this formula its credibility. We have the luxury of overthinking so many things in life, and in so doing, we can analyze many things to the point of ineffectiveness. Let's not do that with this. Because when you fix your eyes on Jesus, all those things in your peripheral vision have a tendency to become a little more unfocused. Even, and most especially, when the thing in your peripheral vision is yourself.

Fix your eyes on Jesus when . . .

- You cannot stop focusing on the depth of your own sin.
- You feel insecure when considering what people think of you.

- You long for the popularity of someone else.
- You question whether or not you have said the right thing at the right moment.
- You second-guess every conversation.

Again and again, fix your eyes on Jesus, because he is big enough to fill your gaze. There is, in fact, an occasion in Scripture that I think models this well for us. And fittingly, that example comes not from a seasoned disciple, but from a child.

Loaves, Fish, and Un-Self-Conscious Little Boys

The disciples were facing a seemingly insurmountable issue in John 6. Jesus was attracting quite a following in those days, and as frequently happened, a large crowd followed him hoping to see some of the miraculous healings they had heard so much about. Jesus, upon seeing the size of this crowd, asked a question, already knowing what the answer would be. The people (at least five thousand and probably twice that number) were hungry, and so Jesus asked: "Where will we buy bread so that these people can eat?" (John 6:5).

The disciples, who had seen the miracles firsthand, who had been walking with Jesus for some time, looked at each other with big eyes. They all knew what Philip put into words: "Two hundred denarii worth of bread wouldn't be enough for each of them to have a little" (v. 7). In other words, even with an entire year's salary to devote to the task, the crowd could only have a bite.

That's when the story takes a turn. They did not have the bread; they did not have the denarii; and as it turns out, they also didn't have the faith. But there was one among them who had something—a small boy who presented his meager lunch of five barley loaves and two fish to get the ball rolling.

Perhaps you remember the end of the story. Jesus used the gift of this little boy to feed a multitude. In fact, he used it to do more than feed the multitude. When all the people were fed and when all the leftovers were collected, there were twelve basketfuls that remained uneaten—one basket for each of the disciples to take home as a souvenir.

It's a great story, but here's the thing: Are we to believe that this boy was the only one in the crowd who had remembered to pack a lunch for the day? Probably not. Surely there was a conscientious mother somewhere on the hill who had a package of crackers in her purse. So where were all the other volunteers?

We can't say for sure, for the Bible does not. Maybe their food was spoiled. Maybe they were selfish and didn't present it. Maybe this boy was simply the one closest to Andrew and so his lunch box got chosen. We don't know, but maybe . . .

Maybe the adults in the crowd had the same attitude as the disciples. Maybe they looked at the size of
the crowd and what they had to offer and were simply
too embarrassed to even bring it up before Jesus. Maybe
their self-consciousness got the better of them and they
decided to keep their lunches to themselves: *This isn't
enough. It's not even worth putting out there. I don't have
anything valid to offer. Somebody's going to laugh at me
if I walk up there carrying this.* Driven inward by that
self-consciousness, they were paralyzed into inaction
and silence.

Sound familiar? It certainly does to me. The foil
for these disciples—these followers of Jesus who were
quickly becoming educated (at least in their own
minds) about the things of God—was a child who
was just innocent enough to believe that Jesus would
actually accept and do something amazing with what
seemed so insignificant and small.

It makes me think of the picture of Jabba the Hutt
that hangs on the wall in my office. My son gave me
that picture when he was three years old. If you were
to examine it today, you could find any number of
things wrong with it. "Jabba" is misspelled. He certainly
wasn't green in the movies. And there is some pretty
extensive coloring outside the lines at play there. But
my son gave me this picture, and he did so with all the
joy and pride that only a child can.

But now my boy is growing up, and he doesn't give me pictures very often these days. It's not because he doesn't still draw; he certainly does, and he's pretty darn good at it. He rarely gives me his creations anymore because he doesn't want to give me something that he doesn't think is good enough. His self-consciousness has started in on him, and as a result, he has begun to sec-ond-guess how his father might respond when presented with such a meager gift.

If we are to grow down, we will bring our badly colored pictures to God. Our measly fish and broken bread. Our weak faith and our inconstant prayer life. We will, like children, bring these to him because we believe that the One we are presenting them to is bigger than our weakness.

Oh, to forget myself and be lost in the grandeur of Jesus. Oh, to regain the sense of wonder that charac-terizes little children who haven't yet grown into that self-conscious sense of foolishness. We must regain this sense of wonder that motivated a little boy to bring his normal, little lunch box to Jesus and see what hap-pened. We must not be too grown up to believe.

CHAPTER 10

FROM BUSYNESS TO REST

From the House to the Car

There is, for most every parent I know, a seemingly insurmountable hurdle in the family schedule that occurs at least once a day. This obstacle is persistent enough and troublesome enough to drive even the most patient of parents to screaming at his or her children. The obstacle is, of course, the great physical, emotional, and perhaps even spiritual void between the time when you say to your kids, "Time to go!" and the time they actually get in the car.

It's amazing to me as a dad how the announcement that it's time to go to school, church, the game, the lesson or the whatever, causes even the most obedient of children to remember all the other things in life that have to be done.

"It's time to go!" But not until the dog is played with.

"It's time to go!" But not until I get another drink of water.

"It's time to go!" But not until I finish the homework assignment that's been sitting in front of me for the last three hours.

And the shoes. Lord, the shoes. It takes an act of Congress each morning to get six shoes on six feet and the laces tied or the Velcro smashed.

We've tried all kinds of things in our home to cross this void; to scale this mountain; to hurdle this obstacle. We've set a fifteen-minute timer on the oven clock to go off. We've just left the kids in the house by themselves while we, the adults, went and got in the car. We've threatened, cajoled, bribed, yelled, and everything in between to try and speed up this process, and we have been found wanting. At least for this period of time, the kids are going to operate on their own timetable and their own schedule, as if there weren't important places to go and important people to see and important things to accomplish.

But it also occurs to me that this is a microcosm of something that is generally true about us as we grow up—we get busy. And in our busyness, we get hurried.

And in our hurry, we get frustrated. And our lives become just a series of exhortations to ourselves and others to do more, and to do it more quickly. Hurry, hurry, hurry in all things, because in all things we are busy, busy, busy.

Compare that to the life of a child. A child, who is not the slave to a calendar. A child, who does not find their identity in the number of their activities. A child, who simply lives in the moment and is not constantly rushed toward the next thing. And yes, a child who is in no hurry to get their shoes on to get out the door.

When you begin comparing those two kinds of existences, you will find as I do something greatly appealing about a life less busy. But this kind of life is not characterized by a shirking of responsibilities or constant lateness to appointments; instead, the redeemed kind of un-busyness is a state of rest that comes from living in the knowledge of Jesus' complete work. This is what we can grow down to. It's not simply a matter of cutting activities; instead, as adults, this growth comes through examining the truth behind our overbooked schedules and overburdened lifestyles, and finding rest on the other side.

The Source of Busy

Why are we such a busy people? There are all kinds of reasons. We might say, for example, that technology has added to our level of activity. In the old days, before the days of constant connectivity, we didn't have access to all our relationships at a given moment. We didn't know there was this thing happening across town or that thing happening in the neighborhood. Neither did we have the ability to check our email every ten minutes and therefore be constantly braced for the barrage of tasks and questions that come our way digitally. Ironically, then, our access to others hasn't necessarily increased our productivity or efficiency, but it has instead simply increased our activity.

Or you might say we are busy people because we live (at least in North America) in a day and time of increased specialization and prosperity. Never before have we been able to have things like travel ball, personal art classes, and dance companies for the kids. With each of these things, which are a luxury to be sure, we add another appointment to our weeks.

So there are real, tangible reasons for our busyness. But perhaps there is something deeper as well—something at the heart level that drives our frenetic pace. For while we might complain about the pace of our lives at a given moment, isn't there that little piece of you that glories in your busyness? I know there is for me.

It's not that having a full schedule is wrong, necessarily. The Lord values work, and he values it a lot. We are to make the most of the talents we've been given, and part of doing so means that we are to be involved. My sense, though, is that the "love" part of my hate/love relationship with busyness is not so much about working as unto the Lord, but rather because of something else. Perhaps some deep-seated need that I am looking to my calendar to meet.

If you're like me, one reason you actually love being busy is that at some level, you believe busyness validates you. When I am busy, it means I have things to do, people to meet with, and stuff to accomplish. I am needed; I am wanted. And my calendar tells me so. In our darkest moments, the ones when we are truly alone with our thoughts and we wonder whether or not we are really loved and valued, a full calendar is a tasty placebo that convinces us of our own validity as people . . . at least for a while.

Perhaps that's not you—perhaps you don't need your calendar to remind you that you are a worthwhile person. But maybe you secretly love an overscheduled lifestyle because it helps you deal with the constant fear of missing out on something. Surely if I am this busy, then I must be in the crowd. In the game. Part of the action. If I'm sitting idly, I know that someone somewhere is doing something. And they are doing it without me. But if I'm rushing from place to place, it means I'm included. Sure, I'm not included in everything, but at least there is a reason I'm not—it's that I was included somewhere else.

We might use our busyness to validate our worth. Or we might use it to ease our fear of missing out on something. But we might also actually love our busyness because our busyness makes us feel superior to other people. Oh sure, I'll pay lip service to those who walk at an unhurried pace, but in the end, I enjoy the fact that I'm sprinting past them. It lets me know that I am actually doing something, and I can sit in judgment of those who at least appear to be doing less. We might bemoan our busyness, yet, all the while bolster our own egos with those appointments that give us a feeling of superiority and importance.

Surely there are other reasons—heart reasons—why we are busy. But in the end, they all boil down to the fact that we pack our schedules with things—even good things—and yet they can subversively become a manufactured substitute for that which only Jesus can truly bring.

Validation.

Justification.

Satisfaction.

Security.

If that is true—that our busyness is not so much a result of our calendars as a result of our hearts—then it's on the heart we must focus. We can deal with the calendar, but the calendar is only a symptom of the true disease that runs much deeper. What we need, more than a vacation, more than cutting back, more than making better use of our time, is rest.

True Rest

No other society in history has planned for and enabled rest like the one we live in. We have built in periods of rest like weekends, have unionized and collectively bargained our way into paid vacations and medical leave acts, and have erected monuments in the form of theme parks that pay tribute to the family vacation. Despite these things, though, most of us are overrun, overstressed, and under-rested. Time is a precious commodity—one we can't seem to really get a handle on, despite our best efforts.

Perhaps that's because just as we have failed to diagnose the true source of our busyness, we have failed to understand what true rest actually is. The writer of the book of Hebrews is helpful to us in this, providing both a glimpse into the source of our pace of life and consequently the antidote for it:

Therefore, since the promise to enter his rest remains, let us beware that none of you be found to have fallen short. For we also have received the good news just as they did. But the message they heard did not benefit them, since they were not united with those who heard it in faith. For we who have believed enter the rest, in keeping with what he has said:

> So I swore in my anger,
> "They will not enter my rest,"

even though his works have been finished since the foundation of the world. For somewhere he has spoken about the seventh day in this way: "And on the seventh day God rested from all his works." Again, in that passage he says, "They will never enter my rest." Therefore, since it remains for some to enter it, and those who formerly received the good news did not enter because of disobedience, he again specifies a certain day—today. He specified this speaking through David after such a long time:

> Today, if you hear his voice,
> do not harden your hearts.

For if Joshua had given them rest, God would not have spoken later about another day.

Therefore, a Sabbath rest remains for God's people. For the person who has entered his rest has rested from his own works, just as God did from his. Let us then make every effort to enter that rest, so that no one will fall into the same pattern of disobedience. (Heb. 4:1–11)

In this passage, we see the writer identify the true enemy of rest, and it ain't technology; it's not over-commitment; it's not disorganization or an inability to say no; it's not even general busyness; it's the thing behind all those things. The true enemy of rest is unbelief. It's because of our unbelief that we look to our calendars to validate us as people, that we are afraid of missing out on something, and that we find our superiority in our calendars.

Long ago, the Lord had a promised land for his people. It was a good land—one with the fields already planted and the houses already built. It was the land of rest, and it was there for the taking. But taken it was not, because the people did not believe the promises of their God. Despite his care, despite his provision, despite his miracles and deliverance, they did not go on because they thought the giants were too big and the weapons were too strong. Back in those days, the children of Israel had the opportunity to cross into the Promised Land, believing that God had secured it for them, but instead they wandered in the wilderness for four decades, simply because they did not believe.

Let me say it again: they did not rest because they did not believe. Rather than resting, they wandered until an entire generation had spun their wheels into the ground and became dust. Living in a state of unrest can feel just like that, it seems; you are on a constant treadmill, exhausting yourself, and yet never going anywhere. But if this passage is true, then the answer to the issue of rest is not merely a calendar change or putting your phone away. Those things are important, but they don't really go to the source of what we need. Instead, we must realize that, like the Israelites of old, we are prevented from entering the true rest of God by unbelief. To see this with me, push past the symptoms of busyness that have overcrowded your life. When you do, you'll likely find some of the same uncomfortable things I have about myself:

- I can't put my phone away because I have an inflated sense of self-importance.
- I can't say no to engagements and activities because I'm just insecure enough to believe they'll never ask me again.
- I am at unrest in my relationships because I don't believe those people will still be my friends if I don't impress them.

Time and time again, unbelief is lurking behind our unrest. The only way, then, to move into rest in our activities, work schedules, relationships, and more, is to truly believe. To believe that we don't need to justify ourselves because God has already done the justifying. To believe we don't need to validate ourselves with activities because we are secure in the love of Christ. To believe that we don't need to prove our value because God has shown us just how valuable we are with the death of his Son.

In short, the way we grow down in busyness and grow up in rest is by faith, countering the lies that are perpetuating our incessant need to fill our lives with activity after activity. It is through reminding ourselves that at the cross, Jesus declared, "It is finished!" over all who trust in him, that we shout back at our hearts that overburden our lives with activity that enough is enough.

Rest Is Not . . .

Like the Israelites of old, the reason we do not enter the promised rest of God is not because of an overcrowded schedule, but because of our failure to believe in the God who has finished his work. If that is true, then there are certain other things that we should remember about this state of rest we are meant to enter into as the children of God.

First of all, we should remember that rest is about more than sleep. In Hebrews 4, we don't see rest being equated with taking a nap. Rather, rest is a state of being—a consistent attribute of our lives. It is possible for us to get a night of sleep and not wake up rested. That's because even though our eyes might close, our soul does not. To truly rest, then, we must rest in mind, body, and heart. The only way we do this is by knowing and reminding ourselves over and over again of the news of the gospel. This, and this alone, is where true striving ceases.

We must also be careful not to mistake rest for leisure. This is a tough one because most of the time the whole reason we work is for leisure, first on the weekends and then eventually on into retirement. If that's our mind-set, then our highest aim is a life of leisure, walking along sandy beaches and fairways. That's not rest; it's laziness. The holiness of rest is not an exhortation to laziness.

Neither should we think of rest as being entertained. Everyone likes to stop thinking for a while, but here's the problem: Entertainment is a drug that can dull our senses for a time. It's a means of escape from whatever is causing us worry and anxiety. There's nothing wrong with being entertained, but if we are using entertainment as a means of escape, then we're not truly resting.

While rest is not the same thing as sleeping, leisure, or being entertained, we should remember a couple of things that are true about this state of rest we can enter into. First of all, we should remember that we can be physically exhausted and still rest. If it's true that rest is not so much a specific period of time but a state in which we live, it is possible and even likely that most of the time that we rest we will also be physically exhausted. Again, to see this, you have to look deeper and realize why we constantly live in a state of unrest. Though some of it might be due to simple scheduling mistakes, the bulk of those mistakes come from a refusal to live in light of the work of God through Jesus. When we live in light of the gospel, you might say that even our hardest of work comes out of the deepest of rest. We work no longer to justify ourselves or prove ourselves worthy to some standard, but we work fueled by the acceptance we have in Christ and through Christ alone.

In addition, we should come to see rest as an opportunity for celebration. In Hebrews 4:3–4, there is a reference to the rest of God on the seventh day of creation. We should ask ourselves here why exactly God—the Creator and Sustainer of the universe, the

Source of all there is—rested. Was he worn out? Did he need a break? I don't think so. God rested because God was finished. Everything was done exactly as it should have been done. The rest of God, then, is a celebration of completion; it is born not out of necessity but out of satisfaction. For us, it means that we can live in a constant state of celebration of the finished work of Jesus. Whether we are sleeping or waking, we are always celebrating that it truly was finished with Jesus. In fact, our work in our jobs, as parents, in the community, or even in the yard on Saturday is not contrary to the true rest that comes from Jesus; it is fueled by the rest that comes from Jesus. This is the kind of rest Jesus calls us to. And we must pursue it, for it doesn't happen by accident.

Pursuing Rest

This kind of rest, the kind of soul rest that only comes from and by faith, is not natural to us. While eventually we will all have to sleep, this specific kind of rest must be intentionally pursued. This is the exhortation in Hebrews 4:11: "Let us then make every effort to enter that rest . . ." No one is going to unintentionally slip into a state of rest. What does that pursuit look like? A few things I believe, all of which will make us look more like children and less like overscheduled adults.

First, and most importantly, we pursue this rest by intentionally believing and preaching the gospel to ourselves over and over again. You, literally, speak to yourself. You tell yourself over and over again about the finished work of Jesus. You remind yourself when you're anxious, insecure, troubled, and fearful of what Jesus has done, and you feel the peace of God that comes from his completed work wash over you.

When we do this, that belief influences every area of our lives. We rest in our parenting knowing that God holds the future of our children. We rest in our work knowing that God will provide for our needs. We rest in our marriages because we are open and authentic with each other as we model the gospel. But we rest in all these things only when we make every effort to do so. This is where resting as a state of being becomes a discipline. In other words—and ironically, I might add—we must work hard at resting. We must work to make sure that in whatever we do, we are doing it not to replace or further what God has already done, but because of it.

We preach the gospel to ourselves, but we also take other action to pursue this state of rest. If we are confident in who we are in Christ, we should not be afraid to take a hatchet to our calendar. We should sit with our appointments open before us, and ask a series of difficult but diagnostic questions:

- Which of these obligations do I really want to do?
- Which of these obligations am I only committing to out of insecurity or a need for validation?
- Do any of these obligations rob me of primary duties as a family member or a church member?
- Am I using any of these obligations as a substitute for what should only be found in Jesus?

You take a good, hard look at your calendar, and then you start trimming. Doing so is more than an exercise in schedule management; it's really a reflection of your faith. You are, through this trimming, intentionally putting yourself in a position to trust the Lord and his opinion of you rather than anything else. Can you really rest in God's work on your behalf without the aid of an overloaded calendar? Can I? This exercise will let us both know for sure.

We preach the gospel to ourselves. Then we process the gospel implications on top of our calendars. Then we impose this same grid of diagnostic questions before saying yes to anything else, so that we do not once again overburden ourselves with these self-gratifying obligations. In doing this, we begin to practice the very spiritual action of saying "no."

That's a bit counterintuitive to say, though, isn't it? It's especially difficult when the need that presents itself is something that surely should be done by someone. And yet we must keep a guard on our own souls, and that of our family, to the extent that we are willing to make the difficult decision to deny ourselves the chance to be busier, feel more important, or validate our own worth.

Dance Team and Being Okay

My daughter is not a quitter. She is tough, resilient, and persevering. She is strong and decisive. But she is no longer a ballerina. Neither is she a modern dancer. She has been both of those things in the past, but not anymore.

She took various kinds of dance classes for several years, and though I don't think she ever dreamed or aspired to be the prima ballerina for a famous dance company, I thought she was very good. But she didn't want to do it anymore.

She came to my wife and me as a semester of dance class was ending, saying that she didn't want to take classes again the next year. We questioned her about her motives, making sure she was positive about this choice. And her response was simple and beautiful: "I don't enjoy it too much anymore." So she backed away.

And what does she do now? Many things. She likes to read. She enjoys baking at home. She loves playing with her dog. She likes spending time with her friends and camping. And while we live in a typical suburban community where evenings and weekends are filled with endless practices and travel sports teams, she is content to do what she does and what she enjoys. She somehow, maybe miraculously, does not feel the pressure to conform to the pace of those around her. Why might that be?

Perhaps it's because of her personality. She is a bit introverted and likes things to be quiet and peaceful. But I hope—sincerely and truly—that at least part of the reason she is okay is because she is growing up in an environment where we are, as best we can, trying also to be okay without the dance team. It's a home in which we are doing the best we can to love each other and our interests as they are and not assuming a posture of achievement and pressure. I hope.

I hope, and I learn from my little girl, for how much more does the family we as Christians belong to sit in opposition to this constant rush and frenetic pace? How much more do we have a Father who tells us we have nothing left to prove?

In this family, friends, I'm resting. Or at least I'm trying to. But that doesn't mean I'm not at work. It doesn't mean I'm not physically tired. It doesn't mean

I'm going to have a day of leisure. It means instead that I am going to speak to my soul and say the same words that Jesus offered time and time again: "Peace to you." He offered that greeting then and now for the same reason—that he is risen. And because he is risen, it is finished.

CHAPTER 11

GROW DOWN

What Happened to Susan?

Four children first walked through the wardrobe. Guided by their sister Lucy, Peter, Edmond, and Susan Pevensie found themselves transported from their uncle's home in the country to Narnia—a land where animals spoke, a white witch ruled an endless winter, and everyone longed for the day when Aslan, the Son of the Emperor Across the Sea, would at last return.

So goes the story in the C. S. Lewis classic, *The Lion, the Witch, and the Wardrobe*. Through the seven books in the series, we learn how Narnia was first created, the battles that took place there, and how the Pevensie children came to be the kings and queens of that land. We follow the adventures not only of Peter, Edmond, Susan, and Lucy, but other children as well, all culminating in *The Last Battle*, when all the children that have fought battles in Narnia come back once again to that land. All except one.

Peter, Edmond, Lucy, Jill, Polly, and even Eustace come to the aid of the Narnians, but Susan is nowhere to be found. It was a fact that did not escape the notice of Tirian, the last of the Kings of Narnia, who addressed his question to High King Peter:

> "Sir," said Tirian, when he had greeted all these. "If I have read the chronicles aright, there should be another. Has not your Majesty two sisters? Where is Queen Susan?"
>
> "My sister Susan," answered Peter shortly and gravely, "is no longer a friend of Narnia."
>
> "Yes," said Eustace, "and whenever you've tried to get her to come and talk about Narnia or do anything about Narnia, she says, 'What wonderful memories you have! Fancy you're still thinking about all those funny games we used to play when we were children.'"
>
> "Oh Susan!" said Jill, "she's interested in nothing now-a-days except nylons and lipstick and invitations. She always was a jolly sight too keen on being grown-up."

"Grown-up, indeed," said the Lady Polly. "I wish she *would* grow up. She wasted all her school time wanting to be the age she is now, and she'll waste all the rest of her life trying to stay that age. Her whole idea is to race on to the silliest time of one's life as quick as she can and then stop there as long as she can."[8]

What happened to Susan? The simplest answer is that she grew up. In her grown-upness, she was too mature, too sophisticated, and too educated to think about things like Narnia anymore. With so many other aspects of life to occupy her time, she had relegated this land and her adventures there to fantasy, something that was fine for children to believe in, but something very improper for adults. Such is the way of adulthood. We might gain all kinds of independence, freedom, sophistication, nylons and lipstick, but in the end we find ourselves wanting. For in our gain, we have sacrificed the same thing Susan seems to have let go to the wayside—belief. This is what the child of God must never grow out of. In fact, simple faith, because it is naturally beaten out of us as we grow, is what the child of God must fight for.

Santa Claus and the Centrality of Faith

Many a Christmas movie can be boiled down to the same plot line. A child has lost his or her innocence, thanks in large part to the cynicism of the adults around them, and therefore lost their belief in Christmas, Santa Claus, flying reindeer, and the like. The movie is a narrative about rediscovering this belief for the child, and then seeing the adults actually come along with them as well. In other words, it's about growing down, even when you're all grown up.

It's not dissimilar to what I've argued in this book—that growing up in Christ is about growing down in the patterns of adulthood that keep us from Jesus. Like the adults in the story, we find ourselves beaten down and embittered by the disappointments of life; and it is consequently a great and mighty struggle for us to come back around to the innocence of childhood. But there is a key difference here. And it's not that God is different from Santa Claus.

Don't get me wrong—he certainly is. God does not dole out his presents based on the behavior of good little boys and girls. But the big difference in this case is the relative importance of faith in the life of the child of God.

When we're talking about Christmas, we're talking about a particular season of the year. A child might go through nine months of real life every year paying little attention to whether or not they believe in Santa. Then, once a year, and for a short time, that belief is heightened. Lists are made, cookies are left, and everybody's waiting for the man with the bag. And then January 1 rolls around, and it's back to life as usual. Nothing could (or should) be further from the reality of the child of God. For the child of God, faith is the centerpiece of all things. Our failure to understand the centrality of faith is one of the culprits for our growing out of it.

Think about it like this: Imagine taking a blank sheet of paper and listing everything that's important to you. Family, friends, education, work, entertainment, burritos—whatever. List all those things out on paper. Everything that holds a place of significance in your affections. Then comes the hard part.

Force rank your list. What on that list has truly captured your heart? Your emotions? Your thoughts? Your money? Over and over again, ask that question until you have not just a list, but a numbered list. Then look to see where Jesus ranks on the list. I know what you're thinking: *If he's anywhere except number one on the list, I've got some repenting to do. I better make sure I get Jesus back up to the top at #1.* But this is a mistake.

It's a mistake because Jesus didn't die to be number one on someone's priority list. He died to obliterate the list entirely.

The priority list philosophy is broken from the very beginning because it assumes a level of segmentation that minimizes the rule and reign of King Jesus over every square inch of our existence. If you have, for example, your family and the Dallas Cowboys as two items on the list, they can essentially function apart from each other. Of course, you want family to be rated higher than the Cowboys, but they have little to no relationship to each other except the order in which they fall. But the gospel that changes us from old to new and brings life from death goes much further than that.

Jesus is not the top of the list; he's the center of the wheel.

A better visual, instead of the priority list, would be a wagon wheel. If you picture it in your mind, you'll see several spokes leading out from a central hub. The hub is what gives all those spokes their place and stability, and if a spoke is not locked firmly into the hub at the middle, then it's better used as firewood than a part of that wheel. This is the power of the gospel—it takes a disjointed life of competing priorities and rounds them off in a circular fashion all centered on the same hub that sits at the very center of the cosmos—Jesus Christ.

Of course, in this picture, all those spokes represent different aspects of life. Family, friends, work, relationships, money, movies, food, and everything else has some place in our lives. But each one of those individual aspects of life are not disjointed from some top priority; instead they are all locked firmly in place and given definition by the hub in the middle. And if some aspect of our lives does not fit into the hub of Jesus Christ, then we can know it's time for that particular aspect to either be reshaped or removed completely.

Jesus is not your number one priority; he is instead the Lord who gives shape, definition, and meaning to everything else:

> So if you have been raised with Christ, seek the things above, where Christ is, seated at the right hand of God. Set your minds on things above, not on earthly things. For you died, and your life is hidden with Christ in God. When Christ, *who is your life*, appears, then you also will appear with him in glory. (Col. 3:1–4, emphasis added)

This is how faith is meant to permeate every part of life, born from the very middle of it. Growing out of faith might mean that we have segmented our faith to an edge rather than the middle, just another component, rather than the driving force for all affections, decisions, and motivations that it should be. When we begin to actively fight for faith to be central in our lives, we will see that everything in life can really be boiled down to one simple question: What do you believe to be true about God?

The Great Lie

This is an old question. Very old, in fact. This is really the root question the serpent raised to Eve in the garden, and she and her husband were found wanting in their answer. Revealed in their choice of the fruit God had forbidden, they exchanged the truth about God for a lie. The story starts like this:

> Now the serpent was the most cunning of all the wild animals that the LORD God had made. (Gen. 3:1)

This gives us pause, because when you look at what the serpent said to Eve, it doesn't seem *that* cunning. It actually seems pretty straightforward. But read between the lines with me. Satan is saying something else—something more—than what he's actually saying.

Satan led his attack with a simple question: "Did God really say, 'You can't eat from any tree in the garden'?" It's a twisting of God's Word, to be sure, but there's also something else here. He is causing Eve to focus on the one prohibition God gave to his children. He's moving her to a fixation on the negative—to what she can't have—rather than focusing on the hundreds or thousands of trees she could. The underlying message behind this simple question is this:

God is a miser. He is not generous toward you.

But let's not stop there. If we continue to trace that thought down to the center, we see what Satan was really getting at:

God doesn't really love you. If he did, he wouldn't be holding out on you. But he is. He doesn't want you to be happy, and the way you know it is there's something else out there that he won't let you have.

Now we see the cunning. The craftiness. But let's not stop there, because his cunning is evident in other subtle ways. Think, for example, of the implications of Satan going to Eve instead of Adam. God created the world, and humanity, within certain guidelines and systems. In his design, it was the male who was to lead the home. But Satan didn't go to the male; he went straight to the female.

In this, too, we see the subversive attack of the enemy. He is challenging the authority, wisdom, and plan of God, simply by asking the question to Eve at all.

Then there's the word choice of the snake. If you look back to chapter 2 of Genesis, it's interesting to note that, in this chapter that talks much of the creation of man and his purpose in creation, the name of God reads like this: LORD God.

That is the revealed name of God signifying his dominance, mastery, and power, with the name for God as Creator. And yet here slithers the snake and says, "Did God really say . . ."

Not Lord. Subtly, subversively, the snake strips the authority out of God's name and causes Eve to hold God at an arm's length. A Creator who has no real claim on her or her husband.

Cunning indeed. This is the true genius of Satan, for with each one of these seemingly small choices of words or phrases, he steadily chips away not at the will of the human, but of her belief. That's the real key, isn't it? Satan recognizes that actions spring from beliefs. Always. So if you want to direct action, you must begin with belief:

Maybe God doesn't know what he's talking about.

Maybe he doesn't have authority over me.

Maybe he is holding out on me.

Maybe he doesn't really love me at all.

And the dominoes of a belief system begin to topple. When belief begins to falter, it's only a matter of time until actions follow. And these same questions are the root of all the fear, doubt, greed, and self-preservation that run rampant through adulthood. It's all traced back to the same question: What do you believe about God?

So much of life would be simplified if we were somehow, as the children of God, able to simply take God at his Word. So much frustration, anxiety, and fear would disappear if we were able to hear the voice of our Father through his Word, and then accept that he is telling us the truth. Unfortunately, though, we find ourselves in our "maturity" coming up with all kinds of reasons why our particular situation is an exception.

Jesus Is Not a Naïve Savior

We are very much like Peter in this respect. Mark 8 is a case study in our difficulty to simply believe what God says about himself. It's in this passage that Jesus spoke with crystal clarity about what would happen to him in the coming days:

> Then he began to teach them that it was necessary for the Son of Man to suffer many things and be rejected by the elders, chief priests, and scribes, be killed, and rise after three days. He spoke openly about this. Peter took him aside and began to rebuke him. (Mark 8:31–32)

Sometimes Jesus spoke mysteriously. Through stories that seemed like riddles, Jesus talked about the past, predicted the future, and shed cutting light into the present. Very few people, even those who thought they knew him best, understood most, or even half, of what he was saying at a given moment. But not in this passage.

There were no riddles. No illustrations. No stories about virgins and temples and other such things. Here was just the plain truth of what was coming down the pike very, very soon—Jesus, the One in whom these men had placed all their hope for the future—would be mercilessly slaughtered at the very hands of those whom his disciples were expecting him to conquer. And the clarity was too much for Peter in the moment.

"Jesus? Could I have a word with you?"

Yep—that's Peter. Pulling Jesus aside. And what makes it even more astounding is what this same Peter had done moments before: "You are the Messiah" (Mark 8:29). That was Peter confessing Jesus as the Son of the Living God. But here he is, concerned that Jesus surely has some misunderstanding about what it means to be that Messiah. Surely the Messiah could not be killed. Could not be humiliated. Could not be rejected. Jesus just needed a bit of correction.

And so we shake our heads at Peter—poor, poor Peter—the one who can't seem to get out of his own way so many times in the Gospels. It's amazing, though, how many times I scoff at another only to find the Holy Spirit turning the mirror on me. The truth is, I find myself pulling Jesus aside all the time. It's during all those times when I read something he said or did, and think to myself, *Surely he didn't mean what it sounded like he meant.* Or, *surely this doesn't apply to me in the way it seems to.*

In this way, we are not so much like children who are more than willing to take the word of our parents, simply because they said it was so. Instead, we are more like angsty teenagers who are convinced in their very bones that no one understands them or their unique problems. And that surely, no matter what our heavenly Father has said, he cannot actually expect us to believe it:

> *Don't worry, Jesus? That was fine for people in the first century, but have you taken a look at the world today?*
>
> *Rest in you, Jesus? Nice idea, but you don't understand the kind of pressure I'm under at work right now.*
>
> *Live simply and seek first the kingdom, Jesus? Sure thing. Except for the fact that my phone is constantly ringing and emails are constantly coming in with more and more priorities that have to be attended to.*
>
> *You love me? Fully and completely, Jesus? Okay. Whatever you say. If that's true, then you surely can't be privy to everything I've done in my past.*

Time and time again, we do the same thing as Peter—we pull Jesus aside because our situation is different. Our circumstances are unique. Our struggles are profound. Each and every time, we treat Jesus like a guy with some good ideas in theory, but ideas that simply can't work in a life as complicated as ours.

But Jesus is not a naïve Savior.

Consider this, from Hebrews 4:14–16:

Therefore, since we have a great high priest who has passed through the heavens—Jesus the Son of God—let us hold fast to the confession. For we do not have a high priest who is unable to sympathize with our weaknesses, but one who has been tempted in every way as we are, yet without sin. Therefore, let us approach the throne of grace with boldness, so that we may receive mercy and find grace to help us in time of need.

This passage speaks to the spiritual teenager inside of us that echoes the refrain of "you just don't understand." He does.

Jesus has been tested and tried in every way that we have been, are, and will be. More so, in fact. And yet through all of those temptations, Jesus did the one thing that escapes us time and time again—he trusted in the Word of his Father.

When he was tempted to make himself King before it was time, he trusted in the Word of his Father.

When he was tempted to call down angels to defend him, he trusted in the Word of his Father.

When he was tempted to turn away from the painful road of crucifixion that lay before him, he trusted in the Word of his Father.

Jesus, as the Son of God, believed that he could trust his Father. Because he did, he was willing to take his Father at his Word. And we are the beneficiaries of his commitment. We benefit not only because we are the recipients of his righteousness, but because we can be confident that there is not a single situation that we will encounter in this life in which Jesus does not have understanding. Jesus knows. He understands, even if no one else in the cosmos does. In him, we find the rightful ruler of the cosmos. As such, we find the King who commands. But we simultaneously find the Great High Priest, one who intercedes for us before the throne of God. Remarkably, the child of God does not find in Jesus a naïve Savior, but a Jesus then who both commands . . . and understands.

The incredibly good news for you, Christian, as a child of God, is that you are not an exception. Your circumstances do not add up to something that takes God by surprise or finds the loophole in his Word. Jesus is not taken aback for one single second at what you are facing. But neither does he minimize it. He understands all the pressure, all the hardship, all the difficulty—all the reasons that make it so hard for you to simply believe. He understands it perfectly, and in his understanding, he commands that we trust. Above all other things, we must trust as the children of God.

The Ridiculously Impossible

Madeline L'Engle once remarked, "We try to be too reasonable about what we believe. What I believe is not responsible at all. In fact, it's hilariously impossible."[9] This is the fight for the child of God. It's a fight to believe that which is too good to be true, and yet is.

Throughout this book, I have tried to put forth a vision of what might be—what could be—when the child of God begins to embrace more fully what it means to be the *child* of God. I've tried to show that all of these characteristics that seem to come so naturally to children are waiting to be recovered, but that all of these redeemed qualities also have their foundation in God as our Father. And that's really the crux of this battle—that's the ground level fight we must wage in a thousand ways on a thousand days.

Child of God, will you take your Father at his Word?

No matter how much we might want to make the issues of our lives more complex, they can all be boiled down to this. Such as it has been for millennia, so it is now for us. When we come to our Father, when we listen to his Word spoken over us as his children, everything in our adult selves will try and find an exceptional reason why it cannot possibly be true. And again and again, our Father looks at us with outstretched arms, inviting us back to this core relationship that defines all other things.

We are, in this way, like the prodigal son Jesus described. We have been in the far country. It's the country of grown-up people doing grown-up things on a grown-up timetable, and yet we have found it wanting. There is inside of us an inescapable desire to return to the old land, to the farm, and to our Father, where everything was simpler. Everything was straightforward. Everything was trustworthy. So we start, together, the long walk back to him. And it is indeed a long road.

Here we find ourselves on that journey, each step becoming more familiar. Yes, there are the trees we used to climb at the edge of the property. Yes, there's the old stone wall where we once played hide-and-seek. And there is the start of the grazing lands we used to roam with ease and without worry. Finally, there is the house we knew so well coming into view . . .

And there is our Father. He is not only waiting, he is running to meet us. For we are his children, and he takes great joy in us. He is inviting us in, without equivocation or exception, to come home. To be home.

Can it be true? Is life in his house, on his lands, in his country really all that it seems to be? We have seen the ways of the world, and all the logic, knowledge, and experience we've had there tells us that it cannot be so. But here is our Father, so full of love and so full of confidence, inviting us in.

We are on the doorstep now. Inside there is a party—we can hear the sounds, and the joy is nearly palpable. It's carefree, without inhibition—a celebration only children can muster. All that's left for us is to take the final steps over the threshold.

So we step. We step because we believe, as impossible as it might seem, that this is the realest of the real. This is the truest of the true. Our Father has told us it is so, and we will take him at his Word.

NOTES

1. C. S. Lewis is quoting English writer Dr. Samuel Johnson in *Mere Christianity* (1952; repr., New York: HarperCollins, 2001), 83.

2. Richard J. Foster, *Celebration of Discipline* (London: Hodder & Stoughton, 1998), 1.

3. http://www.theatlantic.com/business/archive/2012/02/adulthood-delayed-what-has-the-recession-done-to-millennials/252913/.

4. John R. W. Stott referencing Emil Brunner in Stott's *The Living Church: Convictions of a Lifelong Pastor* (Downers Grove, IL: InterVarsity Press, 2007), 174.

5. Richard Foster, *The Freedom of Simplicity* (New York: HarperCollins, 1981), 4–5.

6. Thomas Chalmers, *The Expulsive Power of a New Affection* (1855; repr., Minneapolis, MN: Curiosmith, 2012).

7. John Calvin, *Institutes of the Christian Religion*, rev. ed. (Peabody, MA: Hendrickson Publishers, 2008), 4.

8. C. S. Lewis, *The Last Battle* (New York: HarperCollins, 1956), 168–69.

9. Robert Wuthnow quoting Madeleine L'Engle in *Creative Spirituality: The Way of the Artist* (Berkeley and Los Angeles, CA: University of California Press, 2001), 143.